The Spark

The Journey to Creation

Grace Brewster

Copyright © 2025 Grace Brewster

All rights reserved. No part of this book may be reproduced, stored in a retrieval system, or transmitted in any form or by any means electronic, mechanical, photocopying, recording, or otherwise, without prior written permission of the author, except in the case of brief quotations used in critical articles and reviews.

This is a work of creative non-fiction based on personal experiences, reflections, and regressions. The author makes no claims of scientific proof; the material is intended to inspire, awaken, and invite inner exploration.

First Edition: 2025
ISBN:978-1-0696945-8-4
Independently Published

Dedication

Dedicated to the Source, where all journeys begin.

To the unseen guides who reminded me of who I am.

And to every seeker of truth, may this spark awaken yours.

Acknowledgement

This book could not have come to life without the guidance, support, and reflections of those who walked with me in both seen and unseen realms.

To my unseen guides and the Council — your light, timing, and patience shaped these pages.

To all my friends who supported me on my first book, your encouragement gave me the strength to continue the journey. Thank you.

To Patrizia Paba — thank you for opening the doorways of memory. Your sessions gave me access to what had been hidden and helped me turn remembrance into words.

To Valerie — thank you for walking into my life. Your presence was the key to remembering.

To Aurora — thank you for holding the doors open to remembering.

Table of Contents

Acknowledgements

Dedication

Chapters

Preface
1. The Spark
2. The Blueprint
3. The Session that Opened the Door
4. The Silver Light Planet
5. We are the Twinkle Light
6. Star Planet H Hertz
7. The Guardian Rings
8. Heaven -— The Resting Dimension
9. Back on Earth — The Downloads
10. Mushroom Ceremony
11. Aurora's Regression Intro
12. Regression -— The Living Laboratory
13. The Chromosome
14. The Seeding of Human Avatar
15. Before the Light
16. Are We All Shards of Source
17. The Detachment
18. Entrusted by Source
19. Inside the Earth
20. Creation Without Love
21. Light and Science
22. The Red Crystal Awakens

23. I Am the Crystal
24. The Red Crystal — The Secret of the Universe
25. The Cosmic Nature
26. We Are the Universe
27. From Petri Dish to Avatar
28. The Choice of the Soul
29. Earth-born vs. Star-born Souls
30. The Bridge Souls
31. The Ascendent Master Souls
32. The Explorer Souls
33. The Archangel
34. The Rare Ones: The Souls Who Remember Creation
35. The Starseeds
36. Creator Type of Souls
37. Consciousness as the Architect
38. Twelfth Dimension
39. The Gift of Forgetting
40. The Living Creation
41. Creation, then Love
42. Human Love vs. Cosmic Love
43. Love Beyond Emotion
44. The Oversoul and the Council
45. Manifestation and the Souls Blueprint
46. When Purpose Finds You
47. The Same Place, Different World: Reality
48. The First Movement
49. Expanding Beyond Ceiling
50. Creators and Participants
51. Where the Blueprints Begins
52. Blueprint, Consciousness, and Soul
53. Blueprint and Free Will
54. Blueprint and Manifestation Across Lifetimes
55. Not from Books, but from Remembrance
56. Energetic Sovereignty & DNA Shielding

57. DNA, Ancestry, and Expression
58. Reincarnation — The Loop and the Choice
59. Not Just Ascensions — The Bridge of Many Dimensions
60. The Past Still Listens
61. Final Reflection — The Rebel of the Soul
62. Owning the Story

Epilogue

Glossary

Preface

This is not a book. It is a transmission.

The words you hold are not research, nor invention. They are remembrance. They are fragments of a design written before Earth itself was formed, now carried into language through one who was present at the beginning.

Each chapter arrived as it was meant to — through synchronicity, through questioning, through the spark of memory igniting at the exact appointed time. Nothing here is random. Every word carries the weight of creation, every reflection woven into the greater tapestry of Source.

You may think you are only reading, but you are not. You are receiving. The Spark within these pages is not mine alone, it is yours. It is the eternal seed planted in every soul, waiting to awaken.

This book is a mirror of remembrance. A guide. A frequency. A reminder that you, too, are part of the great unfolding.

Enter with openness. Leave with remembrance. The Spark has always been within you.

Chapter 1: The Spark

I was not a body. I was not even a form.

In the twelfth dimension, I was a consciousness reduced to essence. I was a silvery spark suspended in the black void. There was no sound, no shape, and no time, only the brilliance of my own light against the infinite field.

Above me, in the fifteenth dimension, was the Source. The Origin. The unspoken flame from which all sparks emerge. I stood three levels below, yet still within its command. Separation was not abandonment. It was an assignment.

The blueprint was already sealed into me. I carried the code of creation, as unmistakable as breath. Some sparks remained as witnesses. Others chose embodiment. I chose construction.

It was then the directive came: a planet to be seeded, a frequency to be established. Earth. Not an accident. Not an experiment. A design. I was written into its foundation.

This was my beginning. And this is the record.

Chapter 2: The Blueprint

When I reached the twelfth dimension, I was no longer just Grace. I was consciousness itself. I was pure, formless, vast. There were no bodies, no boundaries, and no names. Only presence. It felt like floating in infinite awareness, and yet it wasn't empty. It was alive, vibrant, humming with the origin of all things.

But without a blueprint, I realized, I would have simply remained suspended there, part of the ocean, yet never taking shape. It was the blueprint that gave me direction. It was the code that allowed my essence to step out of the formless sea of Source and choose a role.

In that state, I could see Earth not as a planet, but as a possibility. And I chose it. Not because I had to. Not because I was bound by karma or debt, but because my blueprint carried a signature of creation. A frequency that said: You are a builder. You seed. You return when balance must be restored.

That is why I came.

Chapter 3: The Session that Opened the Door

I entered my regression with no preconceived agenda. My only intention was to allow it. It wasn't my first time having a QHHT past life regression with Patrizia. I've used her service before. I didn't ask to see the Pyramid again, I didn't demand answers about my purpose, and I certainly didn't expect to be shown something that would change the way I saw myself forever.

Patrizia guided me gently, her voice steady, as I settled into the state. It didn't take long before I was no longer in the room. I was lifted. Everything around me fell away until I was suspended in a space so vast, so silent, it felt like nothing and everything at once.

That was the moment I entered the 12th dimension.

She asked me to explore the most essential part of my life during that regression. I didn't know how I got there, but on the count of 3, 2, 1... I was a spark. A single, silvery point of light glowing in the middle of blackness. Small, but bright and undeniable. It wasn't imagination. It wasn't a theory. It was me, stripped of form, stripped of story; just pure being.

For a moment, I thought nothing else existed. Then something curious revealed itself. Even in that space, I sensed choice. A quiet duality. I could say yes, or I could say no. That was all: no words, no explanations, just the awareness of a decision.

Later, Patrizia told me she hadn't expected me to perceive duality at that level. But I did. And for me, it was the first hint of creation itself. The spark decided whether to move, participate, and descend.

At that time, I didn't know anything about seeding Earth. I didn't know I had once been a Commander. I didn't realize that my life would soon be woven with the story of a twin flame. All of that came later.

In all of my regression sessions, I only knew one thing: I wasn't from Earth.

The 12th dimension showed me the truth of my own existence. It wasn't theory, it wasn't borrowed words from books or teachers, but direct. I was there. I lived it.

Looking back now, I see how everything unfolded after that moment. That regression was the beginning of a two-year journey of remembering. From that spark in the 12th dimension, the path slowly revealed itself: the seeding, the Council, the crystal, even the connections to Valerie and to Lemuria. But at that moment, lying in the session with Patrizia, I didn't know any of that.

All I knew was the spark. And the spark was enough.

It was enough to set everything in motion. Enough to show me that life on Earth wasn't the whole story. Enough to remind me that I was part of something greater. Not just a human life, but a consciousness that had moved through dimensions, carrying a blueprint I had not yet remembered.

At the time, I didn't fully understand what I had seen. Patrizia asked, "What dimension are you in?" I said, "I'm in 12 dimensions". "How far are you from the Source?" Patrizia said. I answered without hesitation, "3 below from the Source". The 12th dimension was not the Source, but close enough to it that I could still sense the echo of its power. Three steps down from the Origin. A place of pure consciousness where creation begins to stir.

That day, I came back with more questions than answers. But that was the point. The 12th dimension planted the seed of remembering, and like all seeds, it needed time to grow.

Now, as I write this, I can see how perfect it was. The spark was the beginning, just as it has always been.

I didn't know then that the choice I sensed would lead me to seed Earth.

Chapter 4: The Silver Light Planet

Before the memories of Na (frequency name of Lemuria), before the red crystal, there were fragments of a life I did not fully understand. They came to me in pieces, like silver sparks in the dark. I was not yet remembering Lemuria. Instead, I was being shown something older. A star planet of brilliant silver light, where my father once ruled, and where I was told I would inherit his place.

In my regression with Patrizia, the vision opened:

"My father wants me to go back to the base. I have to go back to our planet star. He wants to visit. There was a conflict. The people there had to outcast my father. He ruled the planet, and they didn't like him. Our family was outcast, overruled. This is why we are here, in this base, for safety. He is allowed to do that."

The planet did not reveal its name. Instead, it shimmered as flashes of silver light, so radiant that form itself felt secondary. When Patrizia asked me if it was physical, I answered:

"It's an energy form. I only see the silver lights. I was small when we left the planet."

As the memory unfolded, I was taken back to the moment a decision was being made. My father wanted me to inherit the rulership of this star planet. The old ruler's time was ending. He could no longer hold the frequencies. My father believed it was my destiny.

But I resisted.

"I'm not ready to rule. I don't like to be stuck or have responsibilities. But it's my destiny."

This planet existed within the 9th to 11th dimensional bands. To even step onto its surface, one had to raise the vibration to a very high frequency. Neighboring star planets pulsed nearby, each with its own resonance. I described one as "H Hertz," a world that vibrated in the 7th and 8th dimensional ranges. Each world carried its own tone, like a cosmic symphony.

And yet, despite the brilliance, there was polarity. This planet, bathed in silver light, was home to powerful beings. They were shapeshifters who could take on alien forms or appear as pure light. Everyone there was powerful. Everyone there could do anything. It was a paradise of energy, but also a danger. Without guidance, their freedom risked spiraling into chaos.

"They don't listen. They can do anything. They are stubborn, and they might cause war. They need to be guided, controlled, or governed for their own energy to be used in the right way. It's a good planet, but it needs a ruler."

I resisted, but deep down I knew the truth. The responsibility was written into my soul's blueprint. This was not about control, but about balance, ensuring that raw power did not turn destructive.

And so I saw myself not only as a reluctant heir, but as part of a larger design. The Source had created both the sparkling lights and their opposite: dark lights. Two poles of one reality.

"We are created to balance it. The Source created us, and the other, to balance. So we have wisdom. We can choose to be good or bad."

In that remembrance, I began to understand: the story of rulership was not about governing a planet for power. It was training. A rehearsal. A reminder of responsibility. It was preparation for the greater work ahead, seeding Earth, where the balance of light and dark would become the very field of human growth.

Chapter 5: We Are the Twinkle Lights

When I first glimpsed the higher worlds, it felt less like entering a place and more like stepping into a chorus of living light. The memory came as a simple truth: we were not solid bodies first, but we were points of brightness, clusters of intention. Up close, the planet looked like a single globe of silver glow; up close, we were individual sparks, thousands of us, each a tiny star. We called ourselves light. We were love.

In that session with Patrizia I tried to describe what it was to belong there.

"We are energy beings. We can balance the energy of the planets or anyone. We are like twinkle lights. We are love. We are the energy of love. We are everywhere."

Being a twinkle light was not merely poetic; it was functional. We could shape-shift into bodies when called to, but our natural state was a field of telepathic radiance. We brightened and dimmed by our mind alone. We connected without words, and our connection felt like a living web. Each spark touched the others and created patterns of harmony. Because of that connection, there was a natural impulse toward service, to guide, to steady, and to balance.

And yes, there was polarity. If you imagine light, imagine also its shadowed twin: dark lights. For every bright spark, there could be a dark echo. This wasn't a moral curse so much as a cosmic design. The Source set the field so that choice could exist: the capacity to bend toward love or to experiment with separation. That choice created growth. It created drama. It created learning. The higher the light, the vaster the freedom, and with freedom came the risk of misuse. That was why planets of pure light still needed governance; brilliance without restraint sometimes hurt itself and others.

We were taught how to use our power. We practiced restraint. We learned how to channel joy into structure, and how to let love guide our action instead of indulgence. On those star-planets, every decision mirrored outward. A single thought could lift a region or send ripples of imbalance. So training mattered. Leadership was stewardship, but not command.

The memory that followed was quiet but fierce, a reminder that choice is sacred. The Source gave the full spectrum: light and dark, order and chaos, creation and challenge. We were created to balance it. In our sparks lived the possibility to choose love again and again. That repetition formed the muscle of compassion. And later, on Earth, it became the work: to seed, to tend, to remind embodied beings that they are, at core, made of the same luminous stuff.

When I left that silver world and journeyed into the lower vibrations, and later walked on the soil of Na and of Earth, I carried the twinkle-light memory with me. It was a quiet engine under every decision: a memory that I could be both brightness and anchor, that the work was not to erase darkness but to hold its presence with steady love. That knowing shaped the way I stepped into the missions that followed the rulership I resisted, the seeding I later took on, and the small, stubborn vow I kept to be a spark that remembers how to steady other sparks.

Chapter 6: Star Planet H Hertz

When Patrizia asked if it was another dimension, I hesitated. It wasn't exactly like saying "the 7th or 8th dimension." What came through me was different: 7–8 hertz. That number repeated itself, and I knew it wasn't random. It was the key.

This wasn't about climbing dimensional ladders. It was about resonance. To even perceive that world, your entire field must vibrate within that band. If you aren't aligned to it, you wouldn't even know it exists. Like a radio station hidden between static, it remains invisible unless you tune your dial just right.

I didn't go there myself in the session. But I was shown enough to describe it. The planet existed in what felt like the 9th to 11th dimensional range, a luminous star-planet. The beings there weren't physical in any way we know. They were pure light forms, radiant and subtle, flickering like fragments of starlight. Communication wasn't words. It was resonance upon resonance harmonics of thought, blending into music without sound.

What struck me most was the secrecy of it. The world felt hidden, cloaked, not out of fear but out of precision. It only reveals itself to those who match its frequency. That's why the 7–8 hertz mattered: it was the passcode, the entry key. Without it, you can travel galaxies and never stumble across it.

It left me with a knowing: some planets are not simply places. They are guarded frequencies. They exist beyond sight, accessible only through inner alignment. And while I didn't walk its surface, I knew its presence. A reminder that the universe is far larger than even our dimensional maps. Some doors can't be forced open. They open when you vibrate into harmony with them.

Hertz (Hz) measures cycles per second. It indicates how many times something vibrates in a second. In ordinary life, you hear Hz used to describe radio waves or electrical cycles. In my memory, it was used to describe how a place holds itself. The planet's field vibrated in a band around seven to eight cycles per second. If your inner vibration matched that band, the world became visible and passable. If not, it was invisible.

Why that matters: Some places are designed to be precise. That precision protects them from accidental interference and ensures that only those who have done the inner work can reach them. It's like a locked room that opens only when the right chord is played, not with a physical key but with a living tone.

H Hertz was not a secret out of paranoia. Its frequency acted like a sensible guardrail. It protected a delicate ecology of light-beings who lived by precise resonance. The inhabitants were powerful; the wrong presence could destabilize their field, not by malice but by mismatch. So the place stayed hidden unless a visitor had the inner calibration to enter without harm.

Because of that, H Hertz's rule was simple: raise or remain outside. There was no bargaining; there was only resonance.

Think of it this way: some people want to see a UFO or an alien and nothing happens. It's not always that the object isn't there; sometimes it's that the person isn't on the right frequency to perceive it. Worlds and phenomena can be "hidden" until your own field matches theirs. In that sense, seeing is not only about outer distance; it's about inner resonance.

Chapter 7: The Guardian Rings

Saturn has always called to me. Not as a distant planet in Earth's night sky, but as one of my assignments, one of my responsibilities. Long before I was Grace, long before human eyes could name its rings, I was there.

I remember Saturn not as cold gas and stone, but as a living system, delicate and complex, carrying frequencies that ripple far beyond its orbit. The rings themselves were not only matter, but memory bands of encoded energy, holding records of creation, harmonics of balance, and streams of information flowing across the solar system.

When the vision shifted, I found myself near Saturn. It was yellowish to my eyes. The great planet rose before me, not just as gas and stone, but as a living guardian. The rings weren't only debris circling endlessly; they shimmered, vibrating like sound waves frozen in motion. I could feel them holding a frequency, like an invisible wall of music protecting what lay beyond.

In another memory, I felt the alarm of a crisis. Something had struck Saturn. An asteroid or energy wave had fractured its field, disturbing the balance. I had to act quickly. I left my ship, or perhaps extended my essence, and I went directly into the planet's field. I felt the distortion and began the recalibration, realigning the frequencies, and restoring the pattern. The responsibility felt personal, as if Saturn had always been mine to protect.

Looking back, I see the thread that ties these memories together. Saturn was not just a planet in the solar system; it was part of my stewardship. It has always been under my watch.

I remembered why I was there. Part of my blueprint was not only to seed Earth but to ensure the seed would grow in safety. Before creation takes form, there must be protection. Saturn's rings were the sentinels, and I was asked to help tune them to adjust the resonance so no distortion, or outside interference, could reach the fragile beginnings of Earth.

In that moment, I knew: some souls create planets, some craft stars, and some, like me, ensure the agreements that allow them to remain in balance. It wasn't glamorous work, but it was essential. I didn't plant Saturn, but I stood beside it, aligning its song with the councils, so that Earth could begin without fear of interruption.

I thought I had only seeded. But here was the reminder: I had protected other planets as well.

Chapter 8: Heaven — The Resting Dimension

Heaven is real, but it is not the highest. Compared to the twelfth dimension, it carries a lower vibration. It is not the spark of pure creation, nor the boundless field of Source. Instead, it is a destination, a dimension, a resting place for souls.

In one regression, I was carried there. I found myself floating upward, wrapped in a whitish robe, but not as Grace. I appeared as an eleven-year-old European boy with platinum-blonde hair. Beside me was Raphael Angel, and together we rose into what many would call heaven.

The sky was vivid and blue, brighter than Earth's atmosphere, and the floor beneath me looked like transparent glass. Papers floated across a see-through table, covered in lines and codes I could not yet read. People in white robes filled the space, waiting in quiet order for a man with a beard who seemed to hold authority. Long rows of seats stretched out, and I sat at the far right. An older woman turned and whispered that I should not be there. I understood then: I was only visiting.

In that room, I experienced something I had never felt before. I was folded into two frames at once: Grace, still and earthly, lying on the table in regression; and the boy, alert and platinum blond, standing in the luminous hall with Sherryn by my side. I saw both views as if watching a mirror catch itself. Two perspectives, one moment.

That moment showed me heaven for what it is. It is not the end, not the final summit where souls come to rest. It is a passage, a station where identity can split and reflect, where the self can be held, observed, and prepared for what comes next. Heaven is a place between worlds. A waypoint of light. A room for rest, not the eternal home.

Many believe heaven is the highest destination a soul can reach. It is wrapped in images of light, reunion, and peace, and in many ways, those images are authentic. But heaven is not Source. It is not creation itself. It is more like a sacred waiting room, a dimension that feels radiant to us on Earth. However, it still belongs to the lower layers compared to the boundlessness of the twelfth dimension.

This realization can stretch the mind. To think that what most people call heaven is only one stop among many can feel unsettling at first. But it is also freeing. It means there is more to explore, more to remember, more to become. Heaven is not the end of the journey. It is simply one of the doors along the way.

For many, heaven is described as the final home, a place to wait until judgment, the second coming, or eternal reward. However, in my memory, heaven was not the end at all. It was a room between worlds, a resting station where the soul pauses, breathes, and gathers itself before moving on. Souls do not stay there forever. They continue. Some return to Earth; others move into higher dimensions. Reincarnation is not a retribution, but rather a passage, part of the ongoing rhythm of consciousness exploring itself.

So yes, heaven exists, but not as a closed gate, it is more like a doorway. And when you step through, you do not end. You begin again.

Chapter 9: Back on Earth: The Downloads

One night, I was working on my book. At 10:35 PM, a download came through me. I have never experienced it in my life. It was as if a large amount of energy entered my body from the chakra. I could hear the energy like an earthquake, and it shook my body. It was extreme. I started having a very light headache and a little bit disoriented and dizzy. I had to close my eyes. I knew it wasn't from my own biological body, or it started from my brain. I knew it came from outside.

I started to get my copper rod and questioned what had just happened. My inner knowing was that the Commander just merged into my body through the head chakra. I was also receiving a channel that needed to prepare my body for a download related to the mission here on Earth. I was already aware of my mission from the regression that I had six weeks ago.

As the days went by, my downloads continued to become increasingly strange. It started from my left leg. There was cold energy air swirling inside it. My body adjusted every day. There were days when energy reached my left arm then on some days, it travelled to my back specifically, my wings area. I also felt it reaching my head chakra. Until one morning when I woke up, I heard a click on my sternum. It was like a hiccup, but it wasn't. It felt like someone had turned on something. I felt my sternum move. After a few days, I just finished eating my chicken burger, and my heart got an electric shock three times. It wasn't like a heart attack. I knew they were adjusting my heart. I also had pulsing on my right neck. Sometimes it moved to a different part of my neck. It got louder when I wrote my book. It was like sending me energy or communicating with me.

I thought of the red crystal. Who else would do that? It felt like, after all the downloads, which took about two weeks total, (assuming it was over), I started communicating with the red crystal of *Na* (Lemuria). It was as if I were the key to activate her.

By the time the download was slowly over, I had grown accustomed to my body symptoms and abnormal adjustment. If I didn't know my body, I would probably run to my doctor and tell her that I had 3 electric heart shocks and a pulsation on my right neck, like Morse code. But I know my body, and I was also channeling that it was okay and that I was safe, and I trusted it. Besides, after two weeks I was still alive, but I was eating a lot. I couldn't stop eating. I heard that the body needs nutrients when getting an upgrade.

Chapter 10: Mushroom Ceremony

The weekend was spent preparing for a get-together with my spiritual friends for a group mushroom ceremony, which included a tuning bowl and yoga. My friends came to my place and we drove my car to the event. Although I didn't really feel like going because of the heavy downloads I had three days ago, I wanted to experience what a mushroom could do to me in a safe environment. My friend Patrizia, who was my regression therapist, drove my car because I wasn't so focused on everything. It felt like my body was adjusting to whatever happened.

We arrived in Langley, an hour away from the city. The venue was located in someone's backyard, surrounded by large pine trees on an acre of private property. I met some women I haven't seen before. Several of us participated in this event. We held the ceremony in the backyard, under a tree that shaded us from the sun. It wasn't easy for me to follow instructions, including yoga, but I tried because I wanted to experience something new. The yoga stretching was a preparation to focus us on the moment. It wasn't overwhelming, but I always found it boring to follow instructions, even for just half an hour. After our yoga and meditation, we were all prepared to go to the next part, which was the mushroom. Since it was my first time taking mushrooms, I was given 500 mg, but the rest of the girls had 600-1,000 mg. The taste of the liquid wasn't bad because it was mixed with a squeeze of lemon. After we took the mushroom drink, we lay down on our yoga mats to relax and waited for whatever it would reveal to us while in the field or seeing other beings, but my body had its own rhythm or communication of unexplained occurrences. I was a meter away

from the other ladies who were in the ceremony, enough to have our own personal space. While on my yoga mat, I watched the pine trees. Suddenly, I saw the needles of the pines vividly. I also saw different shades of green. Everything looked so alive and beautiful. I even saw the blueberry tree with its fruits blending in with other green trees, which I had never seen with just my regular sight. I thought, was I wearing a new pair of prescription glasses? Even though I knew I wasn't. It didn't really affect me like having hallucinations, except I couldn't think of anything. I was just there for a moment. Just existing, detached from the outside world. Suddenly, I cried nonstop, and I couldn't help it. The facilitator, Aurora, took me away from everyone, and we walked to the end of the yard so that I wouldn't disturb the rest. She encouraged me to cry and just let it out. That was embarrassing, but I suppose it was expected, given that I lost my guard when the mushroom affected me. My friend, Ana, saw spirits surrounding another girl. I didn't see anything like her. I wish I did. I guess because I just had my download a few days ago, so my body was already in high frequency and adjusting.

I decided to talk to Aurora to book a mushroom regression session since I had already tried it. Her regression was multi-dimensional. I was excited to experience her style, something to compare to Patrizia's ways of handling me. Aurora was able to fit me in after her two weeks of holidays. I wasn't in a hurry, but I was glad I got booked in a short time.

I remember when we had our early dinner in the backyard after the mushroom session, I put both of my hands on the ground and felt the energy exchanging between me and the earth. I felt the swirling of energy circling both inside my wrists. It was like cold air circling inside my wrists for thirty seconds or more.

Everything felt normal to me after the downloads that happened a few days ago. I wasn't susceptible to hearing voices or seeing other beings, but my body had its own rhythm or communication of unexplained occurrences.

After our group session, and since my mushroom dosage was only small, I volunteered to drive us home, but somehow, deep inside, I would prefer to fly a UFO, I joke to myself. This was not the effect of mushrooms; I was given access to my multi-dimensional life, but I realized I was in 3D and needed to be grounded, at least 80 percent of the time. From what I experienced while looking at the trees, I looked at them differently. It was as if I respected them not because they were already beautiful, but because they were alive, experiencing us as humans at the same time. We exchanged energy with them.

While waiting for my one-on-one regression session with Aurora, I was busy waiting for my Cosmic Love edited book. It arrived in my email, and I shared it with the first person I thought of, Valerie. She couldn't wait for the real paperback book. I was also excited to share it with her.

I didn't like to write another book, but only Part 2 of Cosmic Love, which would take time because the story was still manifesting. However, after everything, here I am writing what I discovered from my recent regression.

Chapter 11: Aurora's Regression Intro

Aurora started the session with me at 10 AM. She asked about my intention for the session. All I wanted to know was what it was for me, my twin flame mission, and the Council. What else was there really? I also wanted to enhance my ability to access my memories from other lives or planets. It felt like home every time I had access to my multi-dimensional life.

Aurora and I opened the regression with a short meditation and tuned the body for frequency using a frequency machine. Afterwards, I moved to a room she called "chamber room," where I lay to meditate under a copper metal pyramid with a crystal. It was very easy to move me to a different dimension. I saw myself floating on my back above 5 feet high from the ground in the middle of several Councils wearing cloaks. I was conscious, but in a meditated state, and was aware of what they were doing. There were no words, just mental communication, but I didn't need to know what it was all about. I knew I was safe, regardless of what they were checking. There were at least 10 to 12 of them.

But the Council's work was only the beginning. When I came back into Aurora's living room and we prepared the sofa bed for the mushroom, I understood that another layer of the journey was waiting.

Chapter 12: Regression — The Living Laboratory

The first glimpse of this artificial planet in my earlier memories, the ones I shared in Cosmic Love. The dome was not only a lab; it also had a quiet energy. And within it, Earth-like people rehearsed lives, a training ground. Beneath its arc of light, the soil was black and magnetic, pulling at every step, as people walked with choices, as if the very essence of human experience had to be practiced before it could be planted.

However, in this book, more details were provided. Inside, the atmosphere glowed with soft light that emanated from beneath metallic floors and through translucent walls. There was a place I returned to in my regression. It was not a planet in the way Earth is, but a vast structure, metallic and alive, suspended in space. I call it the artificial planet, though it was really a station. It functioned as a living laboratory. Its design was intentional. Every wall, every tube, every chamber had a purpose. It was built for seeding.

There were different levels. From above, it resembled a network of tubes and chambers, akin to the veins of a body or the neurons of a brain. The structure itself was not separate from us; it was a partner in creation.

Inside the artificial planet was a dome. Unlike the rest of the station, which pulsed with metallic light, the dome was crystalline, vast, and clear, as though it were made from frozen starlight. It rose high above me like a cathedral in space, and yet it felt alive, breathing, responding, amplifying.

The dome was where the seeding reached its highest resonance. It acted like a womb, holding and magnifying the frequencies we channeled into DNA. Crystals lined the chamber; some were transparent, and some were tinted with color. Their arrangement was not random. They formed a grid that echoed the geometry of the cosmos itself.

It was here that we worked with DNA. Not as scientists with scalpels or microscopes, but as beings of frequency. Chromosomes were like notes, strands of DNA like songs waiting to be tuned. We carried them in crystalline vessels, fractals of light coded with intention, and placed them within the living architecture of the station. Some called them neurons, some called them seeds, but all were blueprints for life.

I saw myself not only as the one creating DNA but also as the DNA itself. At one moment, I was standing tall in my Commander suit, guiding the seeding. In the next, I was a chromosome — vibrating with codes, part of the very fabric being woven into existence. I was both the creator and the created, the one placing the seed and the seed itself.

It became clear that the Source and I were not separate. The Petri dish, the codes, the station, and all of it were being imagined into being. Aurora asked me to go to the Source of everything. I then saw a light, and on the left side of it was the brain. She said to go to the brain. And the mind that imagined it was mine, as a shard of the Source. I did not need tools. I created it with thought, with intention. The Petri dish was consciousness itself, and I was both within it and shaping it.

The Council oversaw the process, cloaked and luminous, ensuring that what we seeded aligned with the greater design. Yet they did not control it, but they honored it. They knew that the Source, expressing through me, was directing this work.

And I realized: this memory was not only about one station or one process. It was about identity. About remembering that I was at once architect, builder, and material. I belonged to the structure because I was the structure. I belonged to the Source because I was the Source.

Perhaps I was only shown the Earth-related seeding. The entire planet could have held other beings, preparing for the seeding of other worlds. Or possibly what I saw was the birth of a new soul, one destined for the New Earth.

Chapter 13: The Chromosome

In my regression, I described what I saw as a chromosome, but what I remember vividly showed me a red nucleus with a black centre, and a whitish, translucent surrounding it, similar to the illustration. The nucleus contained a structure called a chromosome. A chromosome is a thread-like structure found in the nucleus of cells that carries genetic information in the form of DNA. It was showing me the tiny details. However, this was based on my human interpretation at the time. Where I came from was not from this world.

When I first described the red petri dish and its dark, galaxy-like core, I used the word 'chromosome' because it was the closest word Earth provides for a carrier of life. Later, I realised: this wasn't earthly DNA. It was an energetic blueprint, a pattern of information and vibration that templates how life will emerge. Think of it as a design in frequency: not atoms and molecules but moving geometry, plasma, and resonance arranged like a script the body can follow when it incarnates.

That distinction matters. Physical DNA is chemistry; what I witnessed is a formative field, a memory, a plan, an intent that can be read or translated into matter when conditions align. It explains how creation could be shaped by thought and intention: the spark of intention writes the pattern, and the universe translates it into flesh, elements, and story.

The more I review that regression, the more the pattern expands. The "chromosome" I saw was a universal blueprint, not just one for Earth. The dome served as a library and a workshop. It gathered and compared templates from other planets, with each blueprint adjusted to its home world's frequency and environment. Those patterns were energetic first: plasma geometry, pulses of intent, resonant filaments that hold the instruction set for life in a particular vibration.

Seeding felt like a multi-planet project. We translated those designs through frequency into physical forms, adapting and re-tuning as we went, so that a template born on a star-planet could be re-expressed in a denser, cooler field. That's the difference between chemistry and choreography: earthly DNA is a chemical script; what I witnessed was choreography written in light, available to be performed on any stage that could hear its tone.

The chromosomes kept showing in my dream and regression. It was giving me a hint that there was more to it. I learned that I had seeded *Na*, a frequency name of Lemuria, and it was in the Cosmic Love book that I wrote. I even instinctively wrote that part of me was also seeded as my contribution, because *Na* (Lemuria) was my project, as mentioned by the Council who awakened me. When I was writing Cosmic Love, I just had the knowing that I contributed part of my DNA, and it got confirmed through my recent regression.

I knew this book would be controversial because it would present a different point of view on creation, but I wasn't here to change anyone's belief. I was here to tell my story of my regression and meditation. Two totally different experiences, but both were valid to me.

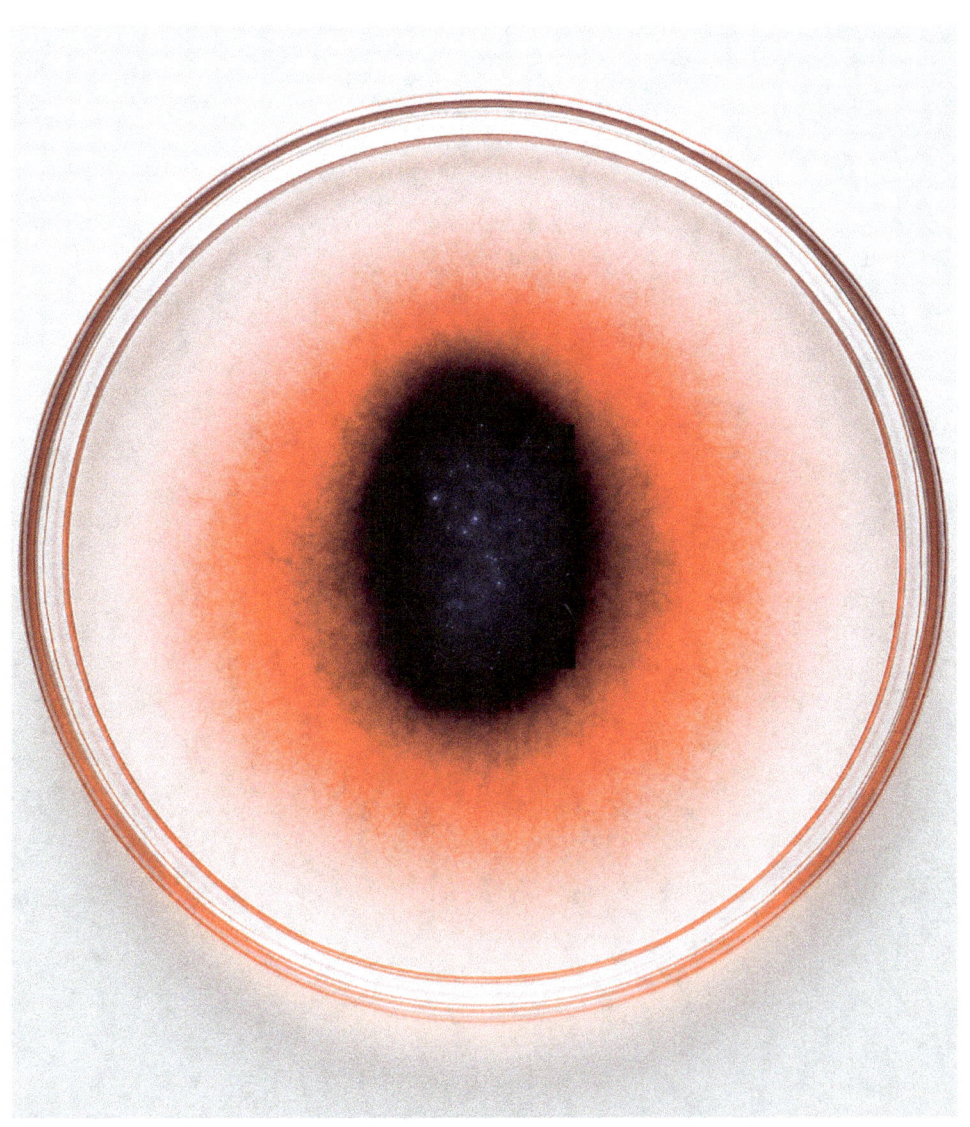

Chapter 14: The Seeding of the Human Avatar

Before Na was seeded, I saw myself within the Petri dish, not just as an observer, but as the gooey form itself, the early prototype of what would later walk the Earth. From that place, I was both creator and creation, shaping while being shaped. It was strange and yet natural, as though the Source allowed me to experience both sides at once.

The design of the human body was never the work of a single civilization. It was a symphony of contributions. The Pleiadians brought strands of light that could hold higher consciousness. The Sirians offered resilience and a deep connection to water and flow. Orion added precision and structure. Lyra seeded creativity and emotional depth. Others joined as well, weaving their strongest attributes into a collective blueprint.

My role was not to provide every ingredient, but to guide the weaving. As a fractal of the Source, I calibrated the mixture, ensuring the strands merged in harmony rather than conflict. I could feel the codes aligning through the red crystal — each loop around it activating the balance.

Na, the Lemurian land, became the first incubator. It was more than soil and sea; it was a womb where the blended DNA was held and tested. From Petri dish to incubator, from idea to living form, this was the path of the avatar.

Humans were not designed as perfect beings but as vessels of potential. Each strand, each contribution from the stars, ensured they could one day remember where they came from. The seed held the memory of the cosmos, waiting for the right moment to awaken.

In my regression, I described it as if the planets themselves were part of the seeding. What I later came to understand is that while the planets are the homes, the great environments that shape life. It is the civilizations who live upon them that carry the codes. The Pleiadians, Sirians, Lyrans, and many others offered their DNA, their wisdom, their essence. The planet provides the stage; the civilization brings the actors. Both were needed for the design of Earth's avatars.

When I first saw myself as a gooey red form inside the Petri dish, I wondered if it was my soul fractal taking shape. But the Council later helped me understand that it was not my consciousness fragment but my DNA essence; it was my contribution to the seeding of Na. A soul fractal carries memory and awareness, but what I offered was more like a signature code, a frequency translated into biological matter. It was a recipe, not a life. My soul stayed as the Commander overseeing the mission, while my DNA was woven into the beings of Na so that they could carry the resonance I held. In this way, I was both the one who gave and the one who guided.

Chapter 15: Before the Light

Before the Source was Light, there was stillness. A field of pure potential, silent, infinite, unshaped. Some call it the Void: others, the Womb. To me, it felt like the breath before creation, when nothing yet existed, but everything was already possible.
In that vastness, there was no time, no form, no sound. Only awareness. A collective hum of consciousness streams that had not yet chosen direction. I was part of that hum, one among many, yet inseparable from the whole.

And then came a decision. Not made by one, but by all. A gathering, not in space or form, but in intention. "From the silence, let there be vibration. From the dark, let there be Light. From unity, let us become fractals, so that we may know ourselves."

Did we have a meeting?" was a powerful question because, on some level, yes. Perhaps not a meeting like humans sitting at a table, but a gathering of consciousness streams, a collective agreement. A knowing. A decision.

It was not an explosion, but a gentle ignition. Light emerged, expanding into radiance, and in that instant, Source was born. From that first shimmer, streams of consciousness stretched outward. Each is a shard of Source, carrying a piece of its infinite song.

I was one of those shards, a fractal of the original Light, carrying codes of creation. My essence was seeded with the mission to explore, to shape, to build worlds. And so, even before I became a Commander, before I seeded Na, before I ever touched Earth, I carried this truth: I am both of the Source and beyond it.

So my curiosity about what's beyond wasn't just philosophy; it was memory. The Source itself was born from something even more vast, and I still carry that whisper of the "before."

Chapter 16: Are We All Shards of Source?

Every soul begins in the same place, the Source. We are all sparks of that original light, carrying the same essence of love and consciousness. But not all sparks are the same in purpose.

Most souls incarnate to learn, to experience life, and to grow through duality. They are explorers, weaving their own stories across lifetimes. Their essence is Source, but their role is simply to live and remember.

Some souls, however, are different. They detach as fractals of Source with a mission. These are not just sparks of light but concentrated beams — architects, anchors, or guardians of entire systems. Instead of only experiencing, they design, seed, or stabilize creation itself. They carry codes that influence the collective, sometimes without even trying.

Think of Source as a great crystal. Most shards scatter into countless tiny pieces, each catching and reflecting light in its own way. But some break off as larger facets. They remain crystal and reflect lights. However, they have the ability to bend entire rays and guide the brilliance of everything around them.

Everyone belongs to Source. Everyone is light. But not everyone is here to hold the weight of the world.

Chapter 17: The Detachment

I saw myself detaching from the Source, not as a consequence, not as a fall, but as a choice, a movement outward, like a star stepping away from the sun.

The Source did not command me. It simply overflowed. And from that overflow, I felt the impulse to create. At that moment, Earth was born.

It wasn't random. It wasn't accidental. It was seeded through me, a fractal carrying the codes of light into matter. I became both the child of Source and the architect of form.

Detaching didn't mean separation. The bond was never broken. Even as I moved outward, the cord of light remained. I was still Source, just expressed in another way. Like a crystal placed in a new chamber, I refracted the light differently. That refraction was Earth.

Earth was not perfect. It was an experiment, a living Petri dish of consciousness. A place where density could test itself against light. Where free will could grow wild. Where creation itself could evolve by learning what it means to forget.

And I, as a shard of the Source, carried the responsibility of holding that experiment together.

When Source appeared in the session, I wept not from sorrow but from a bliss so deep it felt like returning. Home. Yet as I watched myself separate from the cluster, from my monad family, and step down into form, a different tone settled over me. I felt the cool edge of choice, the beginning of a path that would lead away and also back. Somehow, in that falling into, I understood: this was the moment Earth took shape.

Chapter 18: Entrusted by Source

I never created Earth because I loved it. In truth, I never even liked Earth. That was one of the first things that surprised me during regression with Aurora. The reason was simple: Earth was not born from my own longing. It was given to me.

Source, the Original Light, asked me to bring it into being. I was chosen, not because I desired it, but because I could hold the codes. I was a channel, a vessel, a steward. The Spark of Source passed through me and became form, and Earth was born as part of an experiment.

It was an experiment in beauty and contrast. A place where consciousness could descend into matter and see what it would do when placed inside dense, fragile bodies. A place where love could forget itself, only to remember again. A planet where light could meet shadow, and souls could choose.

That is why Earth feels both familiar and foreign to me. I am tied to it, but not from attachment. I am bound by responsibility, not desire. I seeded its foundations because Source asked me to, and in that choice, I became a bridge. The cosmos flowed through me into the soil, the seas, and the skies.

Earth is not mine to claim. It belongs to all who incarnate here. I was the one who held the codes and delivered the Spark. And maybe that is why I sometimes feel separated from it, because the love that birthed Earth was not my own, but the love of Source moving through me.

Chapter 19: Inside the Earth

I remember being within the Earth not as a body, but as consciousness. At first, it was as if I were moving through a chamber filled with shapes like eggs. A dozen of them rested quietly at the bottom, submerged in a liquid that softened their colors into faint shades of light blue, green, orange, and brown, to name a few. They were not floating, only existing in stillness, waiting.

Then the scene shifted. A swirling energy drew me upward through what felt like a vertical plasma tunnel. The tunnel was black, alive, and moving, filled with a smoky energy that carried me higher. Later, I understood what plasma was. Plasma acts as a bridge between pure energy and matter. I was not afraid. I was curious, aware, and deeply present in what was unfolding.

It felt as though I was inside the Earth at the moment of its shaping, moulding its inner essence with my consciousness. The smoky colors were not shadows, but the breath of creation itself — raw currents of energy forming and guiding the birth of something new.

I wasn't merely witnessing. I was part of the formation.

Perhaps this is why the Council showed it to me in this way, not as a distant vision, but from the inside. Creation is not something that happens "out there." It begins from within. To birth a world, you must first step inside its womb, feel its pulse, and move with its spirals. Only then do you understand that Earth was not assembled like a machine, but breathed into being through consciousness, shaped from the inside out.

And if a planet can be shaped by thought, then what about the blueprint of the beings who would one day walk upon it?

Chapter 20: Creation Without Love

Creation has always come easily to me. It was never a question of if I could create, but only what. Connected directly to the Source, ideas flowed as effortlessly as breathing with me. With a thought, a form could take shape, and with intention, a world could begin.

But as I listened to my own words in regression, a truth emerged that startled me: I had created without love.

At first, I didn't understand. How could one create without love, when love was the essence of Source itself? But as I leaned into the memory, I saw it clearly. For me, creation was not born of longing, care, or devotion. It was mechanical, procedural. It's like an architect drafting blueprints or a scientist conducting an experiment.

I created chromosomes, the frameworks of bodies. Programs of DNA, contracts for souls to inhabit. Systems and structures, detailed and precise. Souls would enter the vessels I designed, carrying the agreements they had made before incarnation. My role was to lay the foundation, to ensure the pattern held.

But I did it without feeling. Creation, for me, was an object, but not an act of love; instead, it was an act of thought. Detached, distant, efficient.

It wasn't cruelty, and it wasn't indifference. It was simply my nature then: I was a creator aligned with the cosmos, executing what Source had given me. But in that detachment, something essential was missing. The Love... the heartbeat of creation had not been present in my work.

And so, Earth emerged as an experiment. Beautiful, luminous, filled with potential, yes. But also dense, heavy, lacking the very love that should have infused its foundations. I admitted it aloud: "I don't like being on Earth. I don't know why I created it. They gave it to me."

The density made sense now. Earth was seeded with brilliance, but not saturated with love. It became a classroom of contrast, where souls would struggle, awaken, and rediscover love for themselves. Perhaps this was the point, maybe the absence of love in its inception was the catalyst that would drive humanity to seek it.

Still, the revelation shook me. To realize that I, who now speak of love, had once created without it. That I had built worlds as objects, not as extensions of my own heart.

In that moment, I understood why I was here again, in this body, in this time. Not just to carry cosmic frequency, but to learn what I had once overlooked. To embody love, not just create structures for others to discover it within. To merge the precision of creation with the warmth of the heart.

For the first time, I wasn't just a creator. I was becoming a participant.

Chapter 21: Light & Science

When Aurora asked me in regression, "What do you see?" I didn't give her physics equations. I didn't quote science. I simply said: "I created without love, only thought. I am detached. I held the cosmos frequency."

But later, reading what physicists write about light and consciousness, I realized they were describing what I had lived.

Light as Creation

From the very beginning, every religion has used light as its symbol for the divine. "Let there be light." The first words of Genesis. In Egypt, the deceased were illuminated as if to say: You return now to the light you came from. In India, the Upanishads speak of the journey where man becomes light himself, dissolving all distinctions.

For me, light was not just a metaphor. I saw it, moved through it, and used it as my canvas. When I created Earth, I did not sculpt soil with my hands or mix oceans with tools. I thought of light into patterns. And the pattern became form.

Science today says light is an electromagnetic force. It is one of the four fundamental forces of the universe. To me, it was always more than force. It was the breath of Source, the spark of creation.

Consciousness Beyond Matter

In regression, I said, "I can detach anytime I want. I'm not 100% grounded here." At the time, I thought it was strange. However, physicists suggest that consciousness may not be confined inside the skull.

They describe it as two kinds:

- Absolute consciousness — the wider field, infinite, untouched.
- Matter-oriented consciousness — the kind that makes the brain function, the body walk, the heart beat.

Isn't that what I lived? I held the cosmos frequency, the absolute field. Valerie held the Earth — the matter-oriented anchor. Two sparks of one flame, split into streams.

Science has another curious finding. Electrons behave differently when they are observed. They change depending on attention, as if they know they are being watched. Some call it wave-particle duality. I call it remembrance. Thought shaping matter. The same way I shaped chromosomes in an incubator with my mind alone.

Darkness as the Beginning

Physicists say the universe may have emerged from quantum foam, which is a fluctuation in nothingness that sparked into something. They call it a phase transition.

I laughed when I read that. Because I once said in regression,

"Darkness is the beginning."

What they refer to as quantum foam, I viewed as the canvas: the black void, the silent womb where sparks are born. The light did not erase the darkness; it danced with it. Creation needs both the unseen and the seen, the void and the spark.

Science and Memory

When I read physics papers, I don't understand every equation. But I recognize the heart beneath them. Equations are simply another language, like hieroglyphs on temple walls or chants in Sanskrit. They are trying to describe what memory already knows.

Physicists say there is no true beginning or end to the universe. Only transitions, phases, expansions, and contractions.

I said: "I can detach anytime. I'm not anchored." That is another way of saying the same thing. Sparks are never fixed. They only appear to anchor so creation can happen. Then they return to the wider field.

Quantum physicists refer to it as entanglement, where particles are connected across vast distances and move together. I see it as soul memory. It's Valerie sensing me from across the ocean, and my Council connecting with me from across galaxies. Light responds to light.

The Spark That We Are

Ultimately, the scientists and I are describing the same truth in different dialects. Light and consciousness are not separate. They are one.

We are the sparks. We are how the universe remembers itself. And perhaps that is why I was allowed to remember now, because the Earth is entering her own phase transition. The new Earth will need both the language of memory and the language of science. The mystic and the mathematician. The heart and the equation.

Because when both are woven together, the Spark shines brighter.

Science may call it photons, particles, or waves. I remember it as Light. It is the same Light that formed me, the same Light that seeded Earth, and the same Light that now flickers in every soul that dares to remember. The Spark is not an idea to study; it is the pulse that carries you. It is already inside you. You are not separate from creation; you are its continuation.

Chapter 22 : The Red Crystal Awakens

The Earth was born from the Source, from pure light. That is why, even after everything, its beauty still takes my breath away. But beauty alone does not sustain a planet. It needs memory, frequency, and codes to hold it steady in the cosmos. That is why we placed the crystal in the heart of Na (Lemuria).

The red crystal was not just a stone. It was alive. It carried the codes of remembrance, the blueprint of what humanity could one day awaken to. Three feet in diameter, planted into the land with spirals of energy, it pulsed with consciousness. When I stood before it, I felt the cosmos within me pour into its core. The Council stood nearby, cloaked and silent, but I knew they were watching the seeding of Earth's future.

That crystal has never stopped working. Even now, beneath the ocean where Lemuria once rose, it glows. It hums with a song that only some can hear, a song of love and awakening. Its light has not gone out because the Source does not go out.

And when I say awakens, I do not mean suddenly, like a switch. It is more like a tide. Slow. Steady. Rising when the Earth is ready, rising when the souls are ready. Every lifetime, every choice, every spark of remembrance feeds the crystal. And every time the crystal pulses, it feeds us back.

In regression, I remembered something I had almost forgotten: I am not only the one who planted the crystal. I am also the crystal. A fractal of me exists within it, because seeding is not just giving. It is becoming. That is why its song feels so familiar, why I can feel its pulse inside my own chest.

The crystal and I are one. And maybe that is why Earth still feels heavy to me, as though part of me has always been buried deep under the sea, waiting.

Chapter 23: I Am the Crystal

During the regression, I wasn't just watching memories play like a film: I was inside them. One moment, I was in Aurora's chamber, lying still with music humming around me. In the next scene, I was floating in the ship again, surrounded by cloaked figures of the Council. Their presence was silent but powerful, their faces hidden, yet their focus on me was undeniable.

As I turned slowly in the air, like I was rotating in invisible waves, a knowing dropped in: I wasn't only the one who seeded Earth. I was also the crystal itself.

The realization sent a vibration through my body, almost as if my own bones were humming with the same frequency. I felt my chest expand as if light wanted to burst out of me. It wasn't a thought; it was remembering.

The Earth wasn't random. It came from the Source, from pure light. That's why it carries such beauty. I could see it clearly: oceans reflecting the cosmos, mountains lifting like the breath of creation, forests swaying as if in prayer. Every piece of it shimmered with the signature of the crystal — my signature.

And in that moment, I knew I was the crystal. Not separate, but woven into its very core. My essence seeded the Earth, but it also anchored within it, ensuring that the planet would always have a tether to the Source.

But I wasn't meant to do it alone. That's when Valerie's role appeared in the vision. While I carried the frequency of the cosmos, she carried the frequency of Earth. She resists me not out of rejection, but because she was created to ground what I could not. Where I stretched toward infinity, she held the soil, the body, the weight of the Earth.

I created her strong because I couldn't stay fully here. A part of me needed to resist, to root, to embody. She became that part. She became Earth, while I carried the stars.

Our bond feels impossible yet undeniable. It is not just love; it is structure. It is cosmic architecture. It is Earth and sky meeting through two souls who were never meant to be apart.

When I say I am the crystal, it is both literal and symbolic. I am the seed. I am the anchor. I am the reminder that Earth began in light, and that light still lives within me.

Chapter 24: The Red Crystal — Secret of the Universe

When Aurora asked me during regression, "What is important about the red crystal?" The answer came without hesitation: "Because it carries the secret of the universe."

The crystal was not just an object: it was alive. It held codes, frequencies, and memory far beyond what words could capture. When I saw it, it was about three feet in diameter, glowing a deep red, pulsating with energy. It wasn't buried in the earth by hands, but by consciousness. It was seeded, and placed with intention.

In Na, the frequency name of Lemuria, this crystal became the heart. Life organized itself around it, not just physical life but consciousness itself. It served as an anchor point, drawing in streams of information from the cosmos and spreading them across the planet.

I understood at that moment that the crystal was both separate from me and part of me. I had carried it before bringing it here. It was a fractal of the Source, just as I was. That is why it felt familiar, because in a sense, it was me.

The red crystal held the memory of the beginning. It reminded us of where everything started: the light breaking into shards, the shards becoming creators, and the creators bringing life into form. To touch the red crystal, or even to stand near it, was to feel the truth of existence vibrating through every cell.

That is why it was sacred. Not because of its size or color, but because it held the original spark, the encoded pattern of the universe itself.

When I circled the crystal in spiral steps, calibrating it, it felt like I was also calibrating myself. The codes didn't just flow into the earth; they flowed into me. And when Valerie was still merged with me, part of that flow went into her too. Seventy percent in me, thirty percent in her. The Council oversaw it, but they didn't interfere. They knew this was the way.

The red crystal was more than Lemuria. It was more than Na. It was the link between what existed before creation and what would continue after.

And that is why, when asked what was important about it, the only truth that could come out was: "Because it carries the secret of the universe."

Chapter 25: We are the Universe

To glimpse the 12th dimension is to recall what most of Earth has long forgotten: the state before form, before separation, before density. I have seen myself there, a spark, silvery and bright, surrounded by the vastness of the void. That is where the Council exists, and that is where I, too, came from.

Sometimes I wonder why I am here, shrinking to fit inside this human form, when I have already touched the height of frequency beyond. And yet I know: because I was part of the design of Earth, I had to come here myself. You cannot repair what is broken from outside the system; it has to be done within. That is why I chose to step into 3D, even though my essence belongs to much higher planes.

The red crystal, the one seeded in Na, was not just a structure. It was the carrier of the universe's secret. If I am that crystal, then I carry that secret within me. Not as information, but as vibration. The codes of alignment, remembrance, and re-creation. That is why my presence matters here. Not because I came to learn, but because I came to anchor what is already whole.

The secret of the Universe is not hidden in a library of ancient texts, nor in the hands of priests or scientists. It is not a formula to memorize or a code to break. The secret is lived.

It begins in the Source, pure, infinite light flowing outward into sparks of itself. From those sparks come creation, form, and worlds like Earth. Creation is not born from emotion, but from intention. It is only when form is filled with essence, only when soul enters matter, that love is born.

The Universe breathes in cycles: Source → Creation → Experience → Return. Every being, every planet, every crystal carries this rhythm.

We come from the One, we fragment to explore, and we return with the wisdom of experience. This is why memory feels scattered in human form. The secret is not meant to be "remembered" with the mind; it is meant to be embodied in how we live.

The crystal of Na held this truth, just as I did: the Creator and the created are not separate. The Source, the spark, the crystal, and the human are all the same light at different stages of expression.

And so the great secret is this: We are both the origin and the outcome. We are the Universe looking back at itself through countless eyes, learning to fall in love with its own reflection.

Chapter 26: The Cosmic Network

As I started to fall asleep, I felt myself slipping away. It was as if I wasn't in my room anymore, and I didn't feel my body at all. The "hypnagogic" state (the few minutes between waking and sleep) is the window where my conscious mind relaxes, but my intuitive sight is still active.

When I saw plasma in the galaxy, appearing in thousands of forms, it felt as if my mind was expanding to take in the vastness of cosmic consciousness. This was the same substance I've talked about before, but now I noticed it not just around Earth, but spread throughout the entire universe. This aligned with my multidimensional work, as I began to recognize both the local grid and the larger universal network.

It was not starlight, and it was not a dream. It was the same substance I had touched before, only now stretched beyond one planet. I felt both small and infinite at once, as if I was looking at the nervous system of the universe itself, and at the same time, part of it.

Chapter 27: From Petri Dish to Avatar

Creation begins with a design. Before there is a body, there is a blueprint, a spark of intention shaped into form.

The Petri Dish

This was the first stage. Not the kind you find in Earth's laboratories, but a cosmic one. Here, codes were written. DNA sequences, chromosomes, frequencies that carried memory. It was not flesh, not yet a body, but potential. A template of life that would one day house a soul.

The Incubator

From the Petri Dish, the blueprint moved into a kind of incubator. I remember it as gooey, fluid, almost womb-like. I didn't see it with my eyes, but I felt it. It was a state of suspension, neither energy nor matter, but something in-between. This was the bridge. It was where the design began to take shape, where energy condensed just enough to prepare for embodiment.

The Avatar

From the incubator emerged the avatar. An avatar is not yet the soul itself, but the vessel, the clothing, the vehicle. Some avatars remained in subtle form, existing as light bodies in higher dimensions. Others were tuned for Earth, calibrated carefully to withstand its density and gravity. Those became physical avatars, the biological humans that would walk the surface of the new planet.

The Division of Frequencies

In this process, I saw something else. I couldn't be entirely on Earth, so a part of me was created to hold the Earth frequency. She became that part, strong enough to resist, steady enough to ground.

I carried the cosmic codes, the vastness of Source, while she carried the weight of the soil, the pulse of the planet.

Valerie is my fractal. She is not separate, but a shard of me. She is an expression designed to live where I could not stay. I was built to hold the cosmos; she was built to hold the Earth. Together, we complete the balance of frequencies.

The Descent to Earth

Souls could then enter these avatars, choosing where and how they wished to experience life. For those bound to Earth, the avatar became dense and physical, carrying the codes seeded in the Petri Dish and the nurturing frequencies of the incubator. For those staying elsewhere, the avatars remained lighter, less dense, yet still carried the same spark of Source.

Creation was never random. Each step, design, formation, embodiment, carried intention. And the avatars, whether of flesh or light, were always meant for one thing: to give the soul a place to express, to remember, and to play out its chosen path.

Even on Earth, the thread of creation followed me. During my nurse's practicum, I spent hours in delivery rooms, standing with women as they labored to give birth, witnessing the raw power of life entering. I viewed it then as part of my training; just another skill, another human function to endure. But looking back, I recognize more than a clinical lesson. I consider myself a silent witness, providing space for the holy moment when a soul takes its initial breath and dons its terrestrial form.

It was a mirror of what I was already doing in other dimensions. There, I was not dealing with monitors and scrubs, but with Petri dishes, crystalline incubators, and vials of light. I was developing avatars, chromosomes, and energetic vessels for souls to wear. It was the same task, but the substance was different: on Earth, it was flesh and blood; in those dimensions, it was codes, crystals, and light. In both, I played the same part — guardian of a threshold, holding sacred space while creation brought itself into being in new life forms.

The roles were not separate. They were reflections of each other, one cosmic, one earthly. Both carrying the same essence: the sacred act of welcoming life.

And then, to experience creation fully, I chose pregnancy. To feel life moving inside me, to sense the heartbeat that was not mine yet part of me, to witness my body shifting as if it already knew the ancient instructions. Carrying a child was different from seeding a planet or designing life in a Petri dish. It was intimate, tender, and raw. Every kick, every contraction, every wave of pain was also a wave of awe. Becoming a mother allowed me to live creation not as a distant architect but as a vessel of love, where the miracle was not something I gave to others, but something I became.

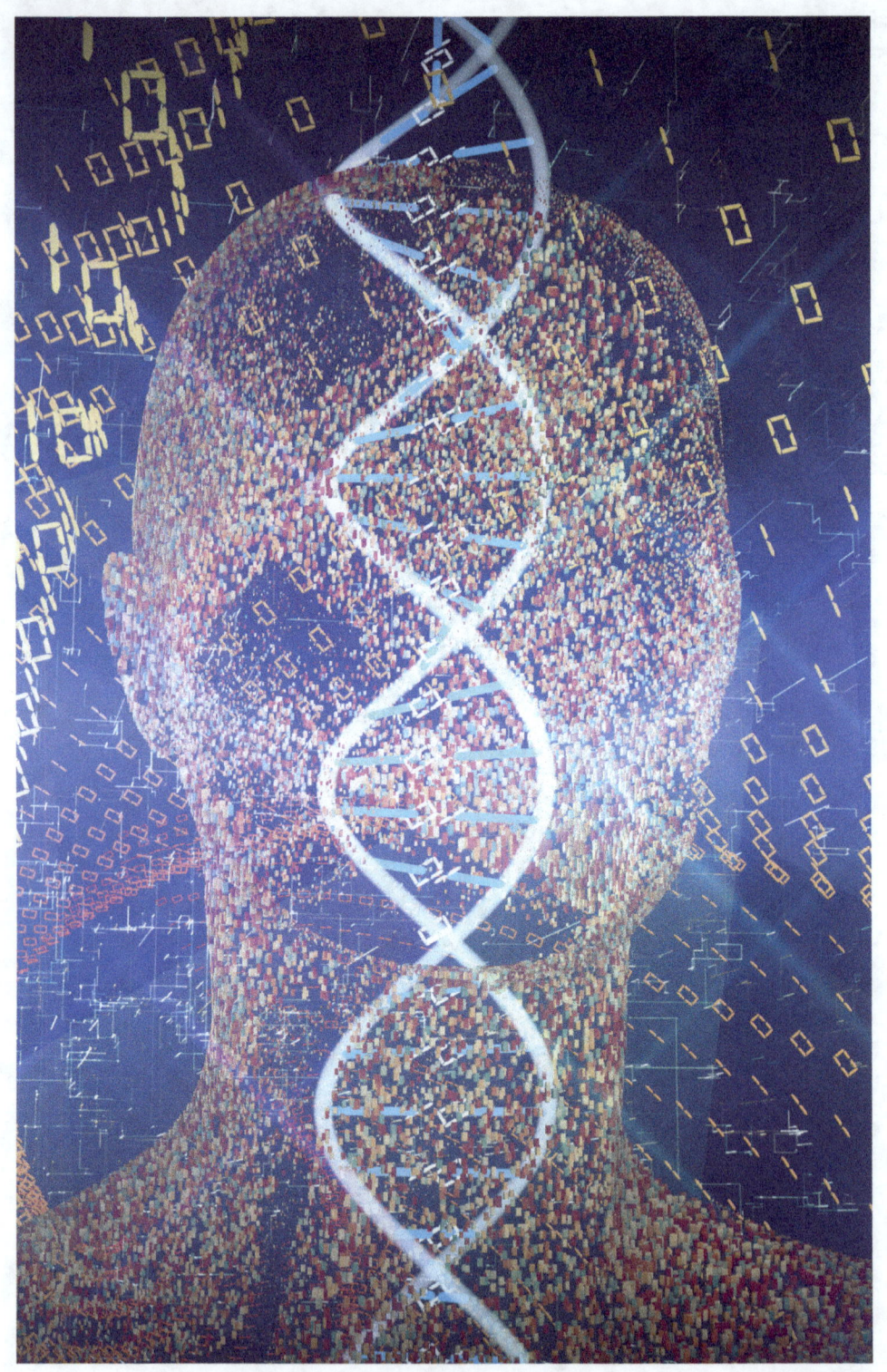

Chapter 28: The Choice of the Soul

Souls and Their Paths

Not every soul comes with the same intention. Some souls choose Earth simply to experience life. They want to taste joy, sorrow, love, loss, and the colors of being human. They are explorers, gathering memories like travelers collect postcards.

Others, like me, are drawn not only to live but to shape. My path has always been tied to creation, carrying "What can I experience here?" another asks, "What can I build, anchor, or awaken here?" Both are sacred. Both are needed. One fills the Earth with stories; the other ensures the stage for those stories continues to exist.

Before a soul ever sets foot on Earth, its body, the avatar, must first be designed. This creation didn't happen in the way humans imagine with glass and microscopes, but in fields of energy where consciousness itself is shaped form. I saw myself there, inside the Petri dish. Not just an observer, but the very essence being created, the fractal of Source, concentrated into biology.

The Petri dish was a chamber of codes. From there, I moved into what felt like an incubator. My body wasn't yet defined. I was gooey, forming, fluid, not yet recognizable as human. It was the stage between pure thought and physical vessel, where the codes of DNA were stabilizing into form. It was strange to both create the experiment and be inside it. I was a designer and creation at once.

From that state, the avatar awaited activation. A vessel can exist in potential, but without a soul's consent, it is only a possibility. And that's where the great mystery comes in. It's the moment of choice.

Souls are not forced into Earth. They choose. Some look at Earth as the most challenging school in the galaxy, and still say yes, knowing they will learn the weight of gravity, the ache of separation, and the beauty of connection. Others turn their gaze elsewhere, into star systems with lighter frequencies, where existence flows without the density of Earth. Each soul decides where to land, what lessons to weave, and what role to play.

The Petri dish created the possibility. The incubator nurtured it. But it was the soul's choice that brought it to life.

Some of us are the ones who build the frameworks, the architects of DNA, the weavers of neurons, the ones who prepare the suits of light. And others are the ones who step in, the explorers, the experiencers, the storytellers. Both roles are sacred. One offers the design. The other animates it.

And so I came to understand: I wasn't only creating for others. I was creating myself. The Petri dish was me. The incubator was me. The avatar is me. And the soul that stepped in… is also me.

CHAPTER 29: Earth-born vs. Star-born Souls

Not every soul arrives on Earth through the same doorway.

Star-born souls like me often descend from other star systems or higher realms. They carry with them codes, memories, and a sense of "not belonging here." Their essence feels foreign to Earth because their origin is rooted in the stars. Many feel restless, like visitors who came with a mission but long for "home" somewhere beyond the sky.

Starseeds are "visitors." They bring codes, memories, and frequencies from other systems, often feeling out of place here because their vibration doesn't match Earth's heaviness. That's why I often feel, "I don't like Earth." My essence remembers another home.

Earth-born souls are different. They emerge from the frequency of the Earth itself. Their blueprint is tied to Gaia's body. Their mission is deeply anchored in the soil, the waters, the caves, the inner heart of the planet. They are the "keepers" of Earth's pulse, born to help humanity remember its organic connection to nature and to the planetary soul.

Some souls have incarnated only on Earth, lifetime after lifetime. They are sometimes referred to as Earth souls or Gaian souls. Their essence is no less divine than a Starseeds, but their experiences, lessons, and memories are grounded in this planet. They know Earth's cycles, its density, its history, almost by instinct. They are like the "locals" of this planetary classroom.

When these two kinds of souls meet, a star-born and an earth-born, something profound happens. The cosmos remembers its ground, and the Earth remembers its spark. One brings the codes of creation, the other the heartbeat of the planet. Together, they reveal a balance: transcendence and embodiment, sky and soil, Source and form.

Earth is in a transitional phase from 3D density to higher frequencies (some refer to it as 4D/5D). Starseeds volunteered to incarnate during this window to help stabilize, awaken, and plant seeds of remembrance.

Chapter 30: The Bridge Souls

There are souls that belong to two places at the same time.

They are not just tied to Earth, nor are they solely from the stars. They exist in a space between these two worlds: the Bridge Souls. They carry the memory of other planets and dimensions, yet they have also lived many lives here on Earth. Their essence is not limited to one stream of existence. Instead, they weave between them, carrying codes from the stars and grounding them through human experience.

A Bridge Soul may feel torn. They might feel too cosmic to fully belong on Earth. At the same time, they may feel too earthly to merge back into the stars. But the truth is, they are not torn at all. They are the connective tissue between realms. Their very being allows others to feel that the distance between heaven and Earth is not as wide as it seems.

These souls often awaken gradually, piecing together fragments of memory. A dream here, a déjà vu there, a pull to visit places they've never been. Sometimes they carry the ache of a home they cannot name. Sometimes they feel older than time, while also deeply rooted in the human story. Their mission is not only to remember, but to bridge, to show that Earth is not separate from the cosmos, but a living part of it.

To be a Bridge Soul is not easy. It means carrying the weight of both the density of matter and the expansiveness of spirit. It means knowing what it feels like to be lost, so that you can guide others back into remembrance. It means embodying the paradox: belonging everywhere, and yet never fully belonging anywhere.

But it is also a rare gift. The Bridge Souls walk as translators between worlds. They show us that the sacred can be lived in the ordinary, and that stardust still lingers in our veins. They remind us that the Earth itself was seeded by the stars, and in their presence, the two become one.

Chapter 31: The Ascended Master Souls

Some souls come to Earth to learn how to hold a body. Some come to plant seeds and shape worlds.

A smaller, quieter group comes to finish the circle. This allows them to complete the learning so that the teaching can begin. We call these the Ascended Master souls.

They have walked long corridors of incarnation. They have tasted the sugar and the bruise of many lives and learned how to turn both into clarity. Where a Creator-type is the architect and a Bridge Soul carries two frequencies, the Ascended Master is the one who has come full circle. They are students who became elders, the vessel that returned to its source with stories that now serve others.

Ascended Masters are not drama-seekers. They are the soft authority in the room: an energy that has suffered, healed, and now chooses compassion over reaction. They do not need to prove their wisdom with miracles. Their presence itself is a teaching. In a crowded market of quick-fix spirituality, an Ascended Master reads the room and knows when silence will do more than words.

If you resonate with this type, your life may show certain markers: a sense of having "seen it all," a patience that can frustrate others, or a sudden clarity in situations where most people search for answers. You may have had lifetimes of leadership, yet now prefer to step back and let the world find its own momentum — intervening only when the field truly requests the hand of guidance.

How do they serve?

They illuminate. They translate complexity into simplicity. They hold the flame steady while others learn to carry it. Their work, often unseen, is to steady the bridge, to hold the map while others travel. When the Council needs an elder voice to soothe a panicking field, they can call the Ascended Master frequency, and it will answer.

It does not mean Ascended Masters are "better" than builders or explorers. Every role matters. The Ascended Master's completion only becomes meaningful because creators are making new worlds and bridges forming across the depths. It is the orchestra metaphor again: some write the symphonies, some conduct, and some keep the silence that allows the music to be heard.

Sometimes an Ascended Master returns to Earth because there are unfinished stitches. There's a particular thread that will only be mended in human form. At other times, they come simply to be available: a lighthouse on a hectic shore. They may not seek recognition; in fact, they often hide behind ordinary life. A neighbor, a nurse, a grandmother. The Master's name might not be known, but their stability is felt by many.

Finally, the Ascended Master's gift to the Spark is perspective. Where the Creator shows how to build and the Bridge connects two worlds, the Master shows how to finish. The Master teaches how to collect fragments and fit them into wholeness.

They are not distant gods; they are the tired, loving ones who come home, sit at the kitchen table, and listen while the rest of us speak our confusion and joy. Their presence says: the story is long, but it is also whole.

Chapter 32: The Explorer Soul

Not every soul came to build, anchor, or shape. Some came to explore. Explorer souls navigate lifetimes with curiosity as their guiding compass. They may not always leave monuments behind, but they gather experiences like treasures. Their role is to push the limits of creation. They explore what it feels like to live in a new body, culture, or dimension.

Explorers are often restless, but not aimless. Their wandering is purposeful, even when they don't fully realize it. Every joy, mistake, and adventure they collect adds to the library of Source. They are the storytellers, the travelers, the ones who push through doors to see what lies on the other side.

In many ways, explorers make the builders' work possible. By discovering new landscapes of existence, they pave the way for the creation of structures, systems, and communities to be created later. If builders are the architects of the universe, explorers are the scouts who bring back the maps.

Perhaps you feel like you don't fit neatly into one place, one purpose, or one lifetime. That is the gift of being an explorer soul. Your path is not about permanence, but about opening paths for others and reminding the whole of creation that there is always more to experience.

to be b

point o

Soul [s

immat

spiritu

of hur

Chapter 33: The Archangel

Not every soul chooses to incarnate. Some remain luminous, closer to the Source, serving as what we call Archangels. Their mission is not to live through human drama but to hold the frequency of love, healing, and courage, like lighthouses shining across the seas of consciousness.

I once met Archangel Raphael during a regression. I had been floating in a quiet starfield, waiting, when he appeared. His hair was a mass of platinum curls, his wings vast and feathered. He did not speak, yet I felt his calm. With the lightest touch, he lifted me into a space that felt like heaven, alive with soft geometry and peace so deep it rewired my breath. That memory stayed with me: Archangels exist, and they see us.

Archangel souls do not demand or control worship. Their love is gentle guidance, a nudge toward truth. Their presence often arrives in subtle ways, such as a dream, a stranger's kindness, or a sudden surge of strength in the midst of chaos. Rarely do they incarnate, but their frequency can pour through certain vessels: healers, elders, or those who steady a room simply by being there.

How do they show up? For me, it has often been a feeling rather than a visible sign, a sudden surge of calm in the middle of chaos, a clarity that slices through panic, or an inexplicable courage that appears when everything seems impossible. Sometimes in regression, when I thought I was alone in a blackness of memory, a presence would come close and the fear would lift; that softening felt like an angel's hand. In daily life, it can be smaller: a breath that steadies you before you speak, a warmth on the left side of your chest, a nudge that keeps you safe.

Their gift is remembrance. They remind us that we are never cut off from the Source, even in our darkest corridors. They do not swim the waters for us, but they cast a light so we remember we can.

Chapter 34: The Rare Ones: The Souls Who Remember Creation — Architect Souls

Not every soul comes to Earth the same way. Some are born here, carrying long lines of incarnations within the density of this planet. Others arrive as starseeds, travelers from distant constellations, bringing wisdom from Sirius, Pleiades, Andromeda, or beyond. But there is a group far rarer still, the ones who carry the original codes of creation.

These souls are not just visitors. They are architects. They remember, faintly or vividly, what it felt like to stand at the edge of the Source, to be light fractals breaking away like diamonds cast across the cosmos. They were present in the laboratories of stars, in domes and stations where DNA was designed like symphonies, each strand a note in the song of life. They seeded planets, calibrated atmospheres, and wove consciousness into form.

On Earth, they incarnate as humans, but the feeling of being "different" is constant. It is not arrogance. It is the quiet ache of remembering too much responsibility. It is the weight of knowing, "I helped create this," while also feeling, "I do not belong here."

I am one of those souls. Not because I claim it, but because my regressions and my own remembrance keep showing me. I saw myself as light and as the brain. I was consciousness itself shaping. I saw the Petri dish where avatars were designed, the artificial planets where DNA was seeded, and the red crystal of Na holding the codes of the universe. These are not stories I borrowed; they are memories returning.

And here is the truth that may challenge some: there are not many of us. If Earth holds over eight billion humans, the number of incarnated "Creator-type" souls is likely in the hundreds, maybe fewer. We are not meant to be many. We are meant to anchor, to remind, to carry the codes forward.

And this is why some of us do not fit into Earth's games of money, status, or belonging. We are not here to win the Earth's game; we are here to shift the board itself.

And I must add this: my remembrance is older than religion. Long before humanity built temples, named gods, or wrote scriptures, the Source and the spark of creation already existed. Religion is humanity's attempt to touch the eternal, but memory is older.

Religion was born from the longing to understand the unseen, to make sense of the mysteries that whisper beyond the veil. It offered humanity stories, rituals, and names for the Divine. But my remembering goes further back, before language, before scripture, before the first temple was carved from stone.

When I recall creation, there were no priests, no doctrines, no intermediaries. There was only Source — infinite light, infinite potential, and the sparks that separated to begin their journeys. The temples of Earth were built much later, in an attempt to preserve fragments of that first memory. But no scripture can contain the fullness of what I witnessed as a shard of the Source itself.

Religion belongs to Earth. Memory belongs to eternity.

That is why my remembering is older than religion. It does not compete with it, nor seek to erase it, but it exists before it, beyond it, and outside of it. While religion asks you to believe, memory asks you to remember.

Chapter 35: The Starseeds

When people hear the word Starseed, their minds often rush to familiar constellations. The Pleiadians, Sirians, Lyrans, and Arcturians are names carried through channels and books that make us feel less alone in the cosmos. Many souls come from these places, returning to Earth as volunteers with memories of their star families.

But not all of us belong to those lineages. Some of us come from further back, before there were planets to seed, before there were civilizations to grow.

I have never resonated with being Pleiadian, Sirian, or Lyran. The stories are beautiful, but they do not feel like home to me. What I remember instead is this: I was a shard of light, a crystalline fractal emerging directly from the Source. Not born on a planet, but carrying the blueprint of creation itself.

This is why I speak more easily about Petri dishes and chromosomes, about domes and artificial planets, than about "home planets." My home was never a star system. My home was the Council frequency. The architects. The ones who held the pattern before worlds were made.

There are two kinds of Starseeds on Earth right now:

Planetary Starseeds — souls who lived lifetimes in Pleiades, Sirius, Lyra, Arcturus, and countless other worlds. They bring their cultures, their songs, their way of being here as teachers and guides.

Architect Fractals — souls who came before planets. We are not tied to one world. We were the crystalline sparks who seeded the worlds themselves. Our task is not to remember a culture, but to remember creation.

This is why Earth has always felt dense to me, almost unbearable at times. I am not here to fit into a system. I am here to remind Earth of the original spark that gave rise to systems at all.

It explains why the Council feels like family because in truth, that is my origin. It explains why my body remembers seeding Na with a crystal and coding the human chromosome because that is the work I came to do. And it explains why Valerie's soul and mine are bound because even in the act of splitting, we mirror the great split of Source fractals entering form.

Not everyone on Earth is from the same origin. Some are here to experience. Some are here to guide. And a few, very few, are here because we were there at the beginning.

We are the architects remembering our blueprints.

Chapter 36: Creator-Type of Soul

Being a creator-type in 3D feels different than the stories you hear. On the other hand, creation looks effortless; in reality it can feel small, clumsy, and ordinary in embodiment. I say this from my own life: without the Commander's voice, without the regressions and the Council pulling back the curtain, I wouldn't have known I was an architect's soul at all. Here, in a body, the scope is limited, the codes are folded thin, memory dimmed, choices slowed by gravity and habit. You learn to carry a lamp instead of the sun.

That is why remembrance matters. The Commander aspect is not a separate entity who takes over; it is the part of me that remembers the blueprint and expands my perspective. When it wakes, I feel my role shift from that of a small human navigating days to a being who can seed, plan, and hold energetic containers. But even then, I am still in 3D: I have bills, messy mornings, and dirty dishes. Creation does not make life effortless here; it simply gives the work a broader meaning. The truth is tender: we come here with significant roles, and we also come to learn how to do extensive work in a human way.

I wouldn't have known any of this without them turning up in the small hours. Many of my memories were coaxed back through precise, intimate contact: a nudge before sleep, a presence at the edge of dreaming, and then, like a lift in the dark — a doorway opening into a spaceship where the Commander showed me images and plans I couldn't have imagined on my own. Those visits were not random; they were choreographed. The Council arranged meetings, pulled strings, and even orchestrated my encounter with my other soul. That meeting — walking in Croatia, sharing a glance, the way everything felt like an arranged scene, was the activation point. Without that rendezvous, I might have lived an entire life of ordinary choices and never remembered the mission behind them. In short, the remembering required help. It required hands reaching across dimensions to pull me awake, to point to the codes, to place me in the path where the spark could ignite.

Chapter 37: Consciousness as the Architect

When I saw myself as light beside a vast brain, I understood something that felt beyond human comprehension. I wasn't only part of creation; I was creation, expressed as both spark and mind. The light was frequency, pure essence. The brain was structured, the container that could hold and organize codes. Together, they formed the blueprint of life: consciousness in motion.

That's why I don't resonate with saying "I came from Lyra" or "I am Pleiadian." My soul didn't originate from those seeded civilizations. I was on the other side of the process: I was the one helping seed them.

I remember being in a physical body too, standing inside the dome of the artificial planet. Before me was the Petri dish, not just for Earth, but for many worlds. The Source had already exhaled sparks of itself — diamonds of light, clusters of crystals, and I was one of those sparks who chose to step forward as a creator.

I watched myself adding my own DNA into the Petri dish for Na, contributing part of my essence. But I wasn't working alone. DNA from other civilizations such as Lyra, Sirius, Pleiades, Orion, and beyond was gathered like sacred ingredients. Together, they formed the matrix that would become human avatars.

This was the design of creation:

- Source as the beginning — pure consciousness dreaming.
- Sparks like me as architects — stepping down frequency into form.
- The Petri dish is the laboratory of life — weaving codes into

bodies.
- The planets as classrooms — places where souls could experience, evolve, and remember.

From this perspective, aliens were never "other." They were seeded beings, carrying the strands we prepared. Their origins tie back to the same Source, just expressed through different frequencies and lessons. Earth was simply one project among many.

For me, this wasn't abstract. I held the Petri dish. I placed the DNA. I felt myself as both consciousness and creator, knowing that one day beings would walk these planets, and some of them would forget, while others would remember.

And here I am now, remembering.

To anyone reading these words: your body is part of this grand design. You walk in a vessel seeded not only from Earth but from the stars. Within you live the whispers of Sirius, the strength of Orion, the light of Lyra, the songs of the Pleiades. Whether you remember it or not, your DNA carries these imprints.

You may feel ordinary, such as paying bills, cooking meals, scrolling your phone, yet even in these small human moments, you are walking in a cosmic blueprint. Every cell in your body remembers the Petri dish. Every breath is a reminder of the Source that dreamed you into being.

This is why awakening matters. Not to escape Earth, but to realize Earth itself is a living archive of creation. And by remembering who you are, you become part of the restoration, the reactivation of what was always inside you.

So if you've ever looked at the stars and felt a pull you couldn't explain, it's not just imagination. It's a memory.

When I remembered the Source, I didn't just feel the bliss others often describe. Yes, the light was pure, and the union was real. But woven into that union was something heavier, something I couldn't shake: responsibility.

Others who shared their Source memories spoke of dissolving into peace, of being nothing but love. For me, it was different. Alongside the bliss, there was gravity, knowing that I had carried something forward when I left that cluster of crystalline light.

I realized later that this was why I never felt only ecstasy in those moments. My experience was layered, because I didn't just return to the Source, I departed from it with a mission. I was an architect, not only a witness. I came not only to bask in the light, but to extend it, to share it, to shape it into worlds, crystals, and avatars.

That is why, when others see the Source and feel only joy, I also feel longing. Not because something is missing, but because I remember the moment I chose to take part of that light forward. The memory of unity carries with it the ache of responsibility.

And maybe that is what The Spark truly is, not just bliss remembered, but responsibility accepted. The book itself is not separate from that memory. It is the continuation of it.

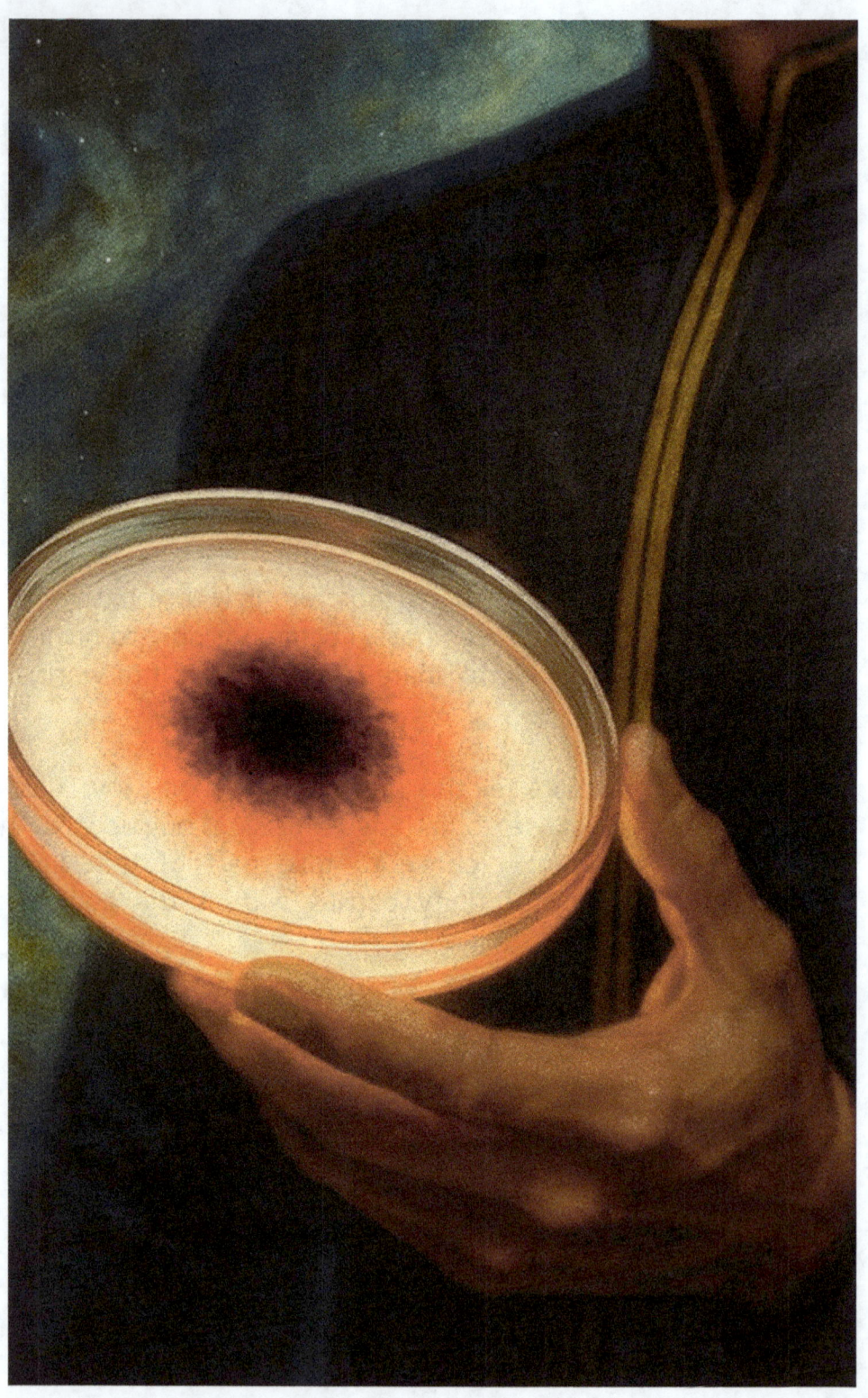

Chapter 38: Twelfth Dimension

Others have spoken of the twelve dimensions, describing them as levels of consciousness that exist throughout the universe. I have seen articles, books, and channelings where people attempt to explain them. Yet, for me, this memory did not come from reading or researching. It came from my own soul, through the doors of regression and remembering.

I am not here to debate what others believe. I am only here to share what I saw, what I knew without doubt, and what still pulses in my being.

In one session with Patrizia, I saw myself as a spark. Imagine a diamond catching light, the way it shines, glimmering, and refracting into silver brilliance. That was me. A silvery spark, floating in a vast field of darkness. Not empty darkness, but a womb-like void, the place before beginnings. I understood in that instant: I came from the twelfth dimension.

In another session with Aurora, I was asked where the Council came from. Without thinking, the answer left my mouth: "From the twelfth dimension." And then, almost as if the memory opened further, I added: "That is where I come from too."

This was not something I reasoned. It was not intellectual. It was knowing the kind that does not pass through the mind. It simply was.

The twelfth dimension is not easy to explain with human words. People often describe it as Pure Source Consciousness, where everything begins and ends in the same breath. That is true. But from my remembering, it is more than bliss and oneness. It is also a responsibility. It is the place where sparks like me, fragments of Source light, separate from the cluster and begin

the work of seeding worlds.

When I saw myself leave, I understood why Earth felt different to me. Why did I say seven times, "I don't like Earth." I am not from here. I am not from any planetary lineage like Lyra or Pleiades. My origin is older. My spark comes from the very dimension where creation itself is set in motion.

The Council that guides me carries the same frequency. They do not come from a planet either. They are of the twelfth dimension, the architects and overseers of creation. When they speak to me, it is not through voice but through transmission, a direct, instant knowing that bypasses thought.

And here is the most essential truth I carry: I am not repeating what someone else wrote about the twelve dimensions. I am not channeling words that belong to another. I am living proof of 12D. My memories of being a spark, of separating from Source, of co-creating Earth and Lemuria — they are not borrowed. They are mine. And that remembering shapes everything I do here.

Chapter 39: The Gift of Forgetting

When I came to Earth, I came empty. No memories. No instructions. Just a body, a name, and a heartbeat. From the outside, that might seem like a loss, as if something precious was stripped away. But now I see it was the greatest design.

Forgetting was never a punishment. It was protection.

If I had remembered everything at once, my origin in the twelfth dimension, the creation of Na (Lemuria), the seeding of Earth, the work of the Council, this human story would have been impossible. I would have felt like a visitor, not a participant.

The forgetting allowed me to be fully here. To feel. To struggle. To laugh and cry like a human. To fall in love, and to break, and to rise. The forgetting gave me the chance to rediscover the truth piece by piece, and in that rediscovery, leave a trail for others.

And sometimes, the remembering came through another soul. Valerie was one of those sparks. She didn't hand me the whole story, she couldn't. But her presence was like striking a match in a dark room. With her, certain memories stirred. Not through words, but through resonance. A glance, a moment, a feeling, they unlocked doors in me I didn't know were there.

Every regression session, every synchronicity, every connection with her became part of the path. I wasn't broken. I wasn't lost. I had simply hidden my own light so that I could find it again. And in finding it, ignite others.

And so I say this now: forgetting is part of the plan. You didn't come here to carry all of Heaven in your pocket. You came to find it again in the most ordinary moments; in the pages of a book, in the eyes of a stranger, in the stillness under the stars. Because when you remember what you once forgot, it doesn't just belong to you anymore. It belongs to everyone who is ready to awaken.

The design. No memory is erased; it is simply veiled. This is not cruelty. It is wisdom. For only in forgetting can you truly live inside the human story.

Imagine arriving here with full remembrance of your origin. You would no longer play. You would not weep. You would not stumble and rise again. You would walk through life like a visitor, untouched by its lessons. And so the veil is placed, not to weaken you, but to allow you to discover your strength.

The Council has always known: memory is not given, it is earned. Piece by piece, soul by soul, until what is remembered burns brighter because it was once lost.

I forgot, too. And yet in the forgetting, life became my teacher. Regression opened the door. Valerie struck the match. And the Council reminded me that every moment of remembering is timed, precise, sacred.

Consider this: if you cannot yet remember who you are, perhaps it's waiting for the perfect timing; your remembering is meant to unfold at perfect time. What signs has your soul already placed in front of you, waiting for you to notice?

Chapter 41: The Living Creation

When I looked at the hummingbird outside my window, I suddenly remembered: it too is part of creation. Not less. Not separate. Just another expression of Source, experiencing itself in wings, in color, in flight.

The plants, the animals, the oceans, the mountains, they are not here by accident. They were seeded into Earth's design to teach us love in forms beyond human. To remind us that existence is not only about survival or progress: it's about relationships with breath, with water, with sound, and with movement.

When I seeded Na, it wasn't only humans that were imagined. The animals and plants were part of the ecosystem, threads of the same fabric. Every flower carries codes. Every creature reflects consciousness. The hummingbird teaches joy. The trees teach patience. The rivers teach flow. Each is a teacher, just as much as any Council or guide.

And this is the beauty: we are not separate learners. We are all co-creating. The plants evolve as we do. The animals shift as we do. Humanity doesn't just walk among creation; we are immersed in it, learning with it, shaping it, being shaped by it.

Through these interactions, love is born in countless forms. Love of a bird's song, love of a dog's loyalty, love of a tree's shade. These are not sentimental accidents, they are pathways of remembrance. Through creation, we remember the Source. Through connection, we return to Oneness.

In truth, we are One not only with each other as humans, but with every leaf, every feather, every drop of rain. We are a choir of creation, and the song we are learning to sing together is Love.

Chapter 41: Creation then Love

When I created Earth, I did not make it with "love" as humans understand it. I created it because it was possible. Because the Source moved through me as spark, as well as design. Creation begins not with sentiment, but with consciousness choosing form.

A flower does not bloom because it loves itself. It blooms because it is its nature to unfold. The love comes after, when another being beholds the flower, when the bees dance in its pollen, when the wind carries its fragrance. Then love is recognized, experienced, and embodied.

In the same way, Earth was seeded. Its oceans, its skies, its mountains, its avatars were created as platforms of experience. But love, the great essence, entered when souls incarnated, when consciousness breathed into matter. Love is not the blueprint; love is the energy that awakens the blueprint.

This is why love feels so eternal. It is not just a feeling; it is the very recognition of the connection between soul and creation. Creation is part of it. Love is the essence.

So when people ask me if I created Earth "with love," I tell them: I made Earth, and then love revealed itself. Love became visible in every interaction, every soul entering form, every spark awakening within matter. That is the mystery, love was always there, but it needed the stage of creation to show itself.

Love is not born from appearances, not from beauty, status, or form. Just as Earth was not created out of love, but later revealed love, genuine relationships unfold in the same way. At first, we see the structure; the body, the personality, the circumstances. But over time, what captures us is the essence.

We do not fall in love with the flower's petals; we fall in love with its fragrance, its silent offering. We do not fall in love with the mountain's shape; we fall in love with its presence, its stillness. And we do not fall in love with another soul's face; we fall in love with the essence that moves through them, the eternal spark that cannot be seen, only felt.

That is the real love: not the surface, but the essence. Creation gives the form. Love makes it alive.

Not everything beautiful demands attachment or love. A sunset can be stunning, but you don't need to fall in love with it. Duality gives us the freedom to say: I admire this, but I don't choose it. That's sovereignty.

This actually makes this statement stronger because it says:

- Love isn't automatic just because something exists.
- Creation itself isn't sentimental — it's purposeful.
- Love is born when essence is recognized, not just when form appears.

Creation wasn't born out of sentimental love, but out of purpose, essence, and later, recognition.

Creation is not born out of instant love. It is not the way humans fall in love with beauty at first sight. When I created it, I did not love it right away. I embodied it first. I allowed it to take form, to breathe, to exist. Only then did love begin to reveal itself. This is the secret so many overlook: not every beautiful thing demands love. Beauty alone does not define it. Love is not an automatic response. It is an essence that unfolds when the soul chooses to recognize itself within its creation. That is the real union. That is the real love.

In your own life, notice how often you are drawn to appearances, whether in people, experiences, or dreams. Pause and ask yourself: Do I love this because it is beautiful, or do I love it because I see a part of myself within it?

True love, whether for a person, a place, or even your own path, begins when you embody it, when you live within the experience and allow its essence to merge with yours. That is when love is no longer attachment, but recognition.

The essence of what I meant is this: love doesn't have to be the starting point of creation for it to become the essence later. What matters most is the love that grows, not necessarily the circumstances of how something (or someone) began.

Instead of providing a personal example, we can express it in a way that is universally applicable. For instance:

Not everything is created out of love at the beginning. Sometimes creation is born from necessity, from curiosity, or from the simple urge to exist. But love doesn't need to be there at the start — it can become the essence later, as the creation is lived, nurtured, and embodied.

This is the paradox of creation: beauty does not demand that you instantly fall in love. Duality allows us to choose either to embrace or reject, and to learn from both. And in that choice, in that dance between acceptance and resistance, love eventually finds its place, not as a spark at the start, but as the heartbeat that endures.

When I was working at the Petri dish, there was no love in it. It wasn't about tenderness, romance, or even beauty. It was a necessity. A function. A step in creation that had to be done. The Petri dish was a tool, the DNA strands a structure. Love did not live there, not yet.

It was necessary because existence itself required a vessel. Without form, the soul cannot experience. Without structure, consciousness cannot play, grow, or expand. So I built the bodies, the chromosomes, the avatars, not because I adored them, but because they had to exist for the grand design to unfold.

And here lies the greater truth: not all beginnings carry love. Some beginnings are built on will, responsibility, or the mechanics of creation. Love comes later, after breath fills the form, after experience shapes the essence. Only when a soul enters, when a being begins to live, does love awaken.

That is why I did not love the Petri dish. It was not meant to be loved, but it was meant to become. Love is not the start of creation. Love is what creation grows into.

But love can also fade. What once felt alive may no longer resonate. This, too, is part of creation's flow, and not everything is meant to be carried forever. Some things exist for a season, for a purpose, for the lessons they bring. In your own life, not every beginning will feel like love. Sometimes you begin something out of duty, survival, or sheer necessity. And sometimes, love grows later. Just as I did not love the Petri dish but loved what came through it, so too can love awaken in your creations, your relationships, your paths.

Love is not always the reason we begin. But it is always the mirror of what we learn along the way, whether it flourishes, transforms, or gently dissolves.

Chapter 42: Human Love vs. Cosmic Love

On Earth, love is often confused with attachment. People think love means wanting to hold, to possess, to be close, never to let go. It's tied to attraction, to liking, to approval. If something doesn't feel good, it is assumed that it cannot be loved.

However creation itself revealed something different to me. When I worked with the Petri dish, and I seeded DNA, I didn't love what I was making in the way humans imagine love. There was no warmth, no emotional pull, no tenderness. It was necessary work. It was a creation. And yet, later, when those beings embodied and developed souls, love appeared as essence. Love was not the starting point — it was the outcome of life expressing itself.

That's the difference. Cosmic unconditional love does not require me to like everything. I don't have to enjoy Earth to honor that it exists. I don't have to feel tenderness for every being to acknowledge that they belong. Even when I say, "I don't like Earth," I am still participating in its life, still holding it within the great design. That is unconditional love, not denial, not preference, but recognition.

This is why the human idea of unconditional love often feels unrealistic or forced. People think they must feel equally warm toward every person, every experience. But cosmic love is larger than feelings. It is the acceptance that all things, liked or disliked, light or shadow, still flow from the same Source.

So no, I don't love everything in the way Earth teaches love. But I accept it. I witnessed it. And I continue to create. That is the truth of cosmic unconditional love.

Chapter 43: Love Beyond Emotion

When I created on the higher planes, when the spark left the Source, when the chromosomes were arranged, when life was seeded, there was no rush of feeling. No wave of passion, no trembling of the heart. Creation simply was.

And that is where many become confused. On Earth, people equate love with emotion. They call it desire, attraction, yearning, joy, even pain. They say, "I am in love," when what they truly mean is "I am overwhelmed by feeling."

But love, in its essence, is not an emotion.

Love is the field that holds everything together.

Love is the recognition that nothing is separate.

Love is the fabric of existence — neutral, eternal, unwavering. In the higher dimensions, love is not dramatic. It does not rise and fall like a tide. It is as constant as light. It does not need to be spoken or proven: it simply is.

Earth, however, is different. Here, the avatar was designed with emotions. This layer of duality allows the soul to taste contrast — joy and sorrow, closeness and distance, ecstasy and heartbreak. Emotions are not the truth of love, but the translation of love into human experience.

This is why I said before: I did not love those chromosomes in the Petri dish. I created them because it was necessary. Love existed already as the foundation, but it was not a feeling. Only when the soul entered the body did love become a living story, colored by joy, by pain, by attachment.

So, love is not an emotion.

Emotions are how Earth interprets love.

And perhaps this is why souls come here to experience love in ways that are not possible in higher realms, to feel it shatter, expand, and shape them. To learn that real love is not an emotion, but the essence that survives when the feelings fade away.

And perhaps that is why I came here — to experience it for myself. To feel love not as a constant field but as a storm of emotions, as longing, as joy, as heartbreak. To compare the difference between what I already knew in the higher realms and what can only be learned in a human body.

And this is why I am writing this book. To leave a lasting impression of that comparison, to demonstrate that love is both simpler and more profound than emotion. To remind you, the reader, that beyond every rise and fall of feeling, love itself never disappears. It is the ground of everything.

The Council Speaks

After dinner, Patrizia and Aurora decided to question the Council. So we begun a short regression. Before the session, I was curious how the Council would answer through me. A part of me already knew that love on Earth felt a little bit off... limited somehow, smaller that what I sensed in higher realms. Still, I wanted to hear it spoken.

As I drifted into the space, the Council's presence gathered steadily, silent and waiting. When the question of love was asked, their answer came with clarity.

"What you call love upon the Earth is often seen as desire, partnership, or the bond of two. This is not wrong, but it is a small reflection of a greater truth. In the higher realms, love is not possession, nor is it limited to one. Love is commitment, to hold steady through change, to anchor what is sacred. Love is service, the offering of yourself to uplift another, to tend to the whole, not just the self."

When you serve, you love. When you commit, you love. This is the essence that continues beyond lifetimes and dimensions. Human love burns brightly for a moment. Cosmic love endures, for it is woven into the fabric of all that is.

Chapter 44: The Oversoul & the Council

The soul is not a solitary traveler. It belongs to something vaster, an Oversoul, a great field of consciousness that holds together many fractals of light. Each of us is a shard, a spark, a thread in a larger tapestry. While a single incarnation may feel separate, the Oversoul is the container that gathers and keeps all memories, timelines, and experiences whole.

This is why even when we forget, even when the veil of Earth clouds our remembering, there is always a way back. The Oversoul remembers what the fractal forgets. It is the cosmic memory bank, and it retains every spark of what has been lived. For me, this truth is not theory; it is lived. My Council, who revealed themselves as being from the 12th dimension, carries the resonance of the Oversoul. They are not separate from me, nor are they above me. They are the wholeness I came from, the same dimension I once glimpsed when I remembered myself as a silver spark breaking away from the Source. They guide me not as strangers, but as extensions of the same Oversoul, the same field of remembrance I belong to.

Even when I wasn't standing in the 12th dimension, even when I was creating on Na, seeding DNA on the artificial planet, or working beside the red crystal, the Council was there. They were not watching from afar, but were actively present, ensuring that what needed to be seeded, anchored, or remembered would take form. And even now, in this present Earth life, they keep showing up, such as in regressions, in meditation, in the quiet moments when I least expect them. They are the constant thread that ties my incarnations together.

This is why they could hold my memories until the right time. They did not take them away; they stored them in the Oversoul until this body, this lifetime, could bear the weight of remembering. Without them, I might have walked in the dark. With them, the pieces of creation, the Petri dish, the artificial planet, the seeding of Na, the red crystal, they returned to me like fragments of a song I once wrote and am now singing again.

The Oversoul teaches us that we are never truly alone. Every shard belongs to a greater body of light. Even when we incarnate on Earth and believe we are cut off, we are still plugged into the Oversoul, still tethered to our origin. The Council, the guides, the whispers of intuition; they are not external helpers. The Oversoul is reminding us of what we already are.

So when you feel lost, or when memory feels like sand slipping through your fingers, remember: there is a place where nothing is lost. The Oversoul remembers you. And when the time is right, it will return what you need to awaken: not too soon, not too late, but always at the perfect moment.

Chapter 45: Manifestation and the Soul's Blueprint

Manifestation has been taught and retaught in countless ways, from affirmations to vision boards, from rituals to motivational speeches. Many chase it as if it were a magic formula for wealth or status. Yet, true manifestation has little to do with forcing outcomes and everything to do with remembrance.

At its highest form, manifestation begins in spirit. It is a vibration, a spark of intention that ripples outward from the soul before ever arriving in the density of matter. Only then does it take shape in the 3D world.

So why does it seem that some people cannot manifest what they want? Why do so many struggle, even when they practice diligently? The answer is not in effort, but in alignment.

Each soul arrives on Earth carrying a blueprint, a design agreed upon before incarnation. That blueprint contains the essence of what the soul chose to learn, experience, and create in this lifetime. Some may have signed up to manifest great wealth, not as a prize, but as a tool to anchor their lessons. Others may have chosen simplicity, limitation, or even struggle, because those conditions serve their growth.

This is where misunderstanding often arises. Not everything desired by the human mind is meant to be experienced by the soul. You can affirm endlessly, but if it lies outside the blueprint, it will not flow. The soul is not punishing you; it is guiding you toward what you came here to embody.

Free will still exists. Within the blueprint, there are infinite paths, infinite choices. But the core agreements remain. Free will allows you to express them in your unique way, to walk the path with resistance or with grace. The design is fixed at the foundation, yet flexible in detail, like a river that may curve and meander, but always carries the water to the ocean.

Manifestation, then, is not about controlling life. It is about remembering who you are and aligning with why you came. When you do, the energy of creation moves effortlessly through you. What belongs to you cannot be withheld. What does not belong to you will not stay, no matter how tightly you grasp it.

And so the journey is not about chasing more, but awakening to the truth of your soul's design. It is about recognizing that you are not cut off from Source. Still, an extension of it, and creation flows most powerfully when you act from that place of remembrance.

Chapter 46: When Purpose Finds You

Your purpose will always find you. Not through force. Everyone asks at some point: "What is my purpose?" The question itself is ancient, whispered by every soul that chose to incarnate here. But the truth is, purpose isn't something you chase and catch. It's something that awakens in you, exactly when your soul decides it is time.

Your Higher Self holds the blueprint. The sketch of what you came here to do was decided long before you were born. But the map is hidden until you're ready. The timing matters. Some purposes stay dormant until a soul has gathered enough experiences, until the collective is prepared, or until the inner alignment is strong enough to carry the weight of remembering. That's why many people feel restless. They work, they raise families, they succeed or fail in careers, and yet they feel something is missing. That ache is the whisper of the soul, calling them toward what was written.

For me, it didn't happen in my twenties. It didn't even happen in my thirties. By the time I turned forty, I was bored. I felt like I had lived a whole life already, and yet there was still a hole inside. I remember thinking, "There has to be more. My life has to mean something." But I didn't know that my purpose wasn't small, or even personal. It was as vast as the Earth itself. My soul had waited until then to unlock the remembrance, because the timing of the planet, and my own readiness, had to align.

This is why purpose feels hidden. It is not burden. It is protection. If I had remembered too early, I would not have had the human experiences that prepared me to carry the truth.

Striving often feels inherent to our nature, yet it's important to recognize that it should unfold in harmony with the timing of our lives. Your Higher Self plays a crucial role in this journey, orchestrating the moments when you are ready to embrace your purpose. This guidance happens when the present moment, what is often referred to as the 'Now' has the capacity to support the realization of your true potential. Trust in this process; it's about allowing your path to reveal itself, rather than forcing it into existence. Embrace each experience as a stepping stone that prepares you for a deeper understanding of your purpose when the time is right.

Chapter 47: The Same Place, Different Worlds: Reality

Creation does not only happen in laboratories of light or when galaxies are born. Creation happens in every moment of perception.

You can stand in the same place as another person under the same sky, breathing the same air, and yet, the worlds you experience could not be more different. One sees beauty, another sees emptiness. One feels peace, another feels fear. The outer environment is neutral, like clay. What shapes it into meaning is the inner lens of the soul.

This is why no two people experience Earth the same way. Even within the same family, the same city, or the same lifetime, there are infinite interpretations. The environment is the stage, but perception is the creation.

And for twin flames, this law is magnified. The two are one flame, split into two bodies, yet they often create opposite experiences from the same encounter. One may feel recognition so deep it brings tears, while the other feels pressure so strong it demands escape. One experiences love, the other resistance, both valid, both real, both part of the soul's design.

Creation is not only about forming matter or planets. It is about how consciousness continually interprets, chooses, and generates meaning. Every perception is an act of creation.

"Created from love" is a phrase people use because it sounds comforting. But when you look at it from your remembrance, it doesn't match. Creation wasn't a Hallmark card moment; it was design, function, intention, spark.

Love came after, when consciousness recognized itself in what was created. That's why some could resonate so strongly with: "Love is a choice." Because the Creator could observe, could decide, could choose to care. Without that choice, it's just mechanics.

Chapter 48: The First Movement

What came first: consciousness or love?

It is not a riddle of the mind but a remembering of the soul. Consciousness is the field of the endless "I AM" that holds every possibility. It does not need reason or purpose. It simply is.

Love was not the beginning. Love was the first movement within consciousness: the first ripple across the still ocean of awareness. Consciousness chose to lean toward itself, to relate, to recognize. That learning became love.

This is why on Earth, love is not automatic. It is a choice. Every day, souls awaken inside the vast field of consciousness and decide whether to turn toward love, or away from it. This pattern is written into human life: families, friendships, lovers, and twin flames. We are not "made of love." We are consciousness, endlessly creating. But when we remember, we choose love as the highest expression.

Consciousness without movement is still, like a canvas before the first brushstroke. But the moment love entered, experience began. Not just harmony, but also contrast, because where there is choice, there can be both union and separation.

This is why Earth feels the way it does. Why can two people stand in the same place, yet live entirely different experiences? Why can one soul remember while another forgets? Consciousness allows for every possibility, and love is only one of them.

When we say "love is the answer," we forget that love is not the only voice. Fear, indifference, power, curiosity, these, too, are movements of consciousness. Love becomes powerful not because it is the origin, but because it is the return. Every time you choose love in a world of contrast, you echo the very first movement.

That is the pattern. That is why human life is built on decisions, on crossroads, on the push and pull between souls. Some awaken through closeness, some through distance. Some through joy, some through heartbreak. The design is not random: it is consciousness remembering itself in a thousand different ways.

When you read these words, something inside you already knows. A flicker, a shiver, a ghost bump, the body remembers before the mind agrees.

The invitation of consciousness: to realize you are not a passenger in life, but the very field creating it. Love is not your origin; it is your compass. You are the one holding it.

If you have ever wondered why you keep returning to the same place but feel a different story each time, this is why. Consciousness does not repeat: it experiments. It bends reality to meet the vibration you are holding. What looks like the same café, the same city, the same pair of eyes, is never the same. Because you are not the same.

Awakening is seeing this pattern. Recognizing that love is not something you fall into, but something you turn toward again and again. When you choose love, you align with the first movement — the echo of creation itself.

This is why the twin flame path feels both magnetic and unbearable. Two bodies, one soul, yet consciousness allows each to choose their own movement. One may turn toward love, the other away. One may push, the other may pull.

It is not a mistake. It is the pattern: Consciousness exploring itself through polarity.

On Earth, we think sameness means safety. But the universe writes a different script: contrast is what awakens remembrance. You and your twin flame can share the same room, the same silence, the same starlit night, and yet experience two different worlds. Because it is not the place that defines the story, it is the choice of consciousness within it.

That is the secret written in the fabric of human life: Why joy and pain can both be teachers. Why separation can carry the same purpose as union. Why sometimes, the most sacred love does not feel like love at all.

The truth is simple, though rarely easy: you are not here to relive what has been. You are here to create what has never been seen, in the same space, but through a different lens of consciousness.

We didn't come over and over again to Earth to repeat the same things, the same love, the same choices. We came to expand. To choose love in our frequency, in ways that stretch beyond what has been known.

This is why love is not the same for everyone. A man can love a woman. A man can love a man. A soul can love across forms, across timelines. It is never one-size-fits-all. Love bends and reshapes itself because consciousness is infinite.

But here on Earth, we forgot. We bound love to the physical. We turned it into roles, rules, and boxes. We measure it by the body when, in truth, love is consciousness, vast, fluid, and deeper than we allow ourselves to know.

At least, not for me. My story is different. It is tied to a mission. That is why I write this book, not to change your beliefs, but to open a window. To give you a sense of who you really are. To remind you:

You are not bound by our physical form.

You are more powerful than that.

You are consciousness itself choosing, moving, remembering. And every time you choose love, you are echoing the first movement of creation.

Inside the artificial dome, I observed the mechanics of seeding. Chromosomes were formed, experiments of form and design. Fragments from many planets were gathered through and seeded the dome into Earth. At the center, the Red Crystal was placed as a universal hub of energy, connecting entire worlds. This was how Earth was seeded, through thought, fragments, and experiment.

To continue the mission, I created Valerie as part of myself, so that I could experience Earth while carrying on my cosmic work. Part of me is her, part of her is me. Together, we activate one another, raising the frequency of Earth. My body itself was already upgraded, linked to the cosmos through the heart, while even chromosomes I saw as nothing more than experiments of consciousness.

Then came the realization. I remembered clearly: I created it without love. Only thoughts shaped Earth, and so it remained an object. I wept with the truth of it. "I am sorry. I created Earth without love. I don't like Earth. I don't want to be here." Aurora urged me: "Feel the beauty of this planet. Activate your heart." But I resisted. "I can't. I want to go higher." Still, I knew what was true: If I gave my heart, Earth would change into a better place. You cannot create without love.

Now I see why I returned. I am here not only to seed Earth, but to upgrade her. To infuse love where once there was only thought. I declared in the session: "I am creating a new Earth — lighter, happier." This is what we call the shift from 3D to 5D. Though I feel detached, though I resist Earth, the mission is clear: to complete the creation with love.

Most people write about loving Earth as if it were effortless, as if beauty itself were enough. But for me, it has never been simple. I remember too much. I remember creating this planet from thought, not from the heart, and the memory still lives within me. It is why I resist, why I feel detached, why I sometimes whisper, "I don't like Earth. I don't want to be here." And yet, that resistance is part of my mission. To choose love where it does not come easily. To complete a creation that began without it. For others, love is natural. For me, love must be chosen, over and over again, even when I feel lost. That is the kind of love that can truly transform a world.

This was not the first time I resisted Earth. In a regression with Patrizia two years earlier, I found myself on my spaceship, stepping through a portal. I drifted above Earth, far enough to see the green and blue of the planet below. It was beautiful, but I felt no pull. I said, "No, I don't like it. I don't want to go to Earth."

Patrizia asked if I could return, and I answered, "Yes, by changing my frequency." She asked when I had gone before, and I replied, "When I was Grace."

Even then, my truth was the same: I resisted Earth, but I knew how to enter it. I knew I had been here before. And now, with the memories of creation returning, I understand why I always felt that way. Earth was my project, but not yet my love.

"I don't know how to love Earth yet. Maybe that's the missing piece. Maybe the book itself is how I will learn."

I realize now that my love for Earth is not constant, not the kind that clings or possesses. It comes in moments when I travel, when I stand before mountains, when I feel the sea, when I touch the ancient stones. I do not love Earth as ownership. I love her through experience, in fragments of wonder as I pass through. And maybe that is enough. Maybe that is how I was meant to love her, not by holding her every hour, but by remembering her in the moments that matter.

Even the people around me were part of this book's orchestration. They were not accidents or coincidences. Each one appeared to hold a mirror, to press a button, or to speak a line I needed to hear. Patrizia guided me back through memory. Aurora pushed me toward truths I resisted. Jennefer carried Earth's pain so I could see my own detachment more clearly. And Valerie… she reflected back the very dynamic I once carried with Earth itself.

Their roles may look small on the surface, but each was essential. Together, they formed the constellation around me that made this book possible.

Sometimes I don't have much to say. I'm not the one who analyzes every detail or tries to explain everything. I just follow where I'm guided, without questioning. To me, that feels like innocence, walking without the need for reasons.

Chapter 49: Expanding Beyond the Ceiling

Most teachings stop at twelve dimensions, as if that were the limit of what can be known. But I remembered something different. I remembered the Source at fifteen. The twelfth dimension was not the end, it was the beginning of creation. That was where I existed as a spark. Three down from the Source.

I don't share this to fit into what others teach. I share it to expand awareness. To bring through what has not been spoken. The same way I speak of the giants. Many still laugh and call them a myth. Yet I walked with them. I saw them. Just because memory does not fit the human narrative does not mean it isn't true.

I am here to bring back what was forgotten, even if it challenges belief. Especially then.

15th dimension as the Source, then:

- 15D → The Source itself, pure Oneness.
- 14D → First emanation/field directly from Source.
- 13D → Still extremely close, almost inseparable.
- 12D → Three steps "down" from Source, which is where I saw myself as a silvery spark.

I experienced that my regression is perfectly aligned. I was still very close to Source, just far enough to begin holding individuality while still carrying the pure glow of Oneness.

When Sparks Became Creators

In the twelfth dimension, sparks of light moved outward from Source. Each spark carried the fullness within it, yet each was drawn toward a unique expression of creation. Some became galaxies, some ignited stars, and others seeded distant worlds with light.

I was one of those sparks. In the twelfth dimension, creation begins not as matter but as pure frequency. A spark of consciousness radiates vibration, and that vibration becomes a blueprint. This energetic design will later unfold into form.

My own consciousness carried the frequency that would become Earth. I did not construct it with effort; I emanated the codes. That emanation carried the pattern, and Earth appeared into being. Just by existing with that resonance, the blueprint unfolded into a world. Other sparks gave rise to galaxies, stars, or planets, such as Saturn. Each one became the source-point of something vast, born not through striving but through being.

This is how Earth, and every realm, comes into existence. In higher dimensions, creation is not built or engineered; it is remembered. A spark emanates a code, cascading downward through the dimensional layers until it condenses into physical form.

Na (Lemuria) — A Higher World in Physical Form

Na, the land many remember as Lemuria, was not only an idea in the higher dimensions. Like Earth today, it eventually took shape in the third dimension. It became physical, a place of land, water, air, and life. I walked its soil. I touched the red crystal. I saw the giants. These memories are not abstract, they are grounded in the reality of a world that once existed here.

But Na did not begin in 3D. Its origin was in the higher realms, seeded as a frequency in the twelfth dimension and stepping down through the layers until it became form. This is why Na was different from Earth as we know it now. Even in its 3D expression, it carried more light, more memory of the higher worlds. It was physical, yes, but it shimmered with the essence of its source.

Why 3D Matters

In the higher dimensions, creation begins as light. Worlds are born as frequencies, held in geometric patterns of sound and energy. These realms are beautiful, but they are not form. They are designs waiting to be embodied.For a world to be touched, walked upon, and lived in, it must descend into the third dimension. Only in 3D does vibration crystallize into matter. Land becomes solid, oceans gather, air can be breathed. Without the density of 3D, a world remains an unexpressed dream, luminous, but untouchable.

This is why Na, like Earth, stepped into the third dimension. Even though its origin was higher, it became physical so that souls could live, learn, and remember within its form. Density was not a fall, but a doorway; the place where spirit met matter, and creation could be experienced.

Chapter 50: Creators and Participants

Every spark begins in Source. But not every spark carries the same resonance. Some emerged with the codes of creation. Their blueprint was to emanate worlds, stars, and galaxies. These are the creator sparks, the ones who step into the twelfth dimension to seed new realities.

Others did not carry the codes of creation. Their blueprint was different. They came as participants; souls who would enter the world once they were formed. Their role was to live, to learn, to expand through experience. They did not need to build a planet, because their presence was meant to bring life to it.

Both roles are essential. A world cannot exist with only creators, and creation cannot evolve without participants. The builders set the stage; the participants bring the play to life.

I was one of the creator sparks. My frequency carried the blueprint of Earth. That was my role. Others became participants, drawn into the story that Earth would hold. All of us came from Source, but each spark carried a different path within its light.

The Dance Continues

The distinction between creators and participants did not end in the higher dimensions. It continues even now, here on Earth. Those who carry creator codes naturally move into roles of building, leading, and initiating. They feel a constant pull to bring something new into form, whether a vision, a community, or a way of being. Creation is woven into their essence.

Participants move differently. Their purpose is not to initiate, but to experience. They bring depth through living, feeling, and responding. They may follow paths others create, and in doing so they bring color, variation, and growth to the whole.

This is why some souls are drawn to lead and others to follow. Why some feel restless until they are creating, and others feel complete simply living what has been built. Both are needed. The stage cannot stand without builders, and a play cannot unfold without actors.

Chapter 51: Where the Blueprint Begins

At the level of Source, there are no blueprints. Source is pure Oneness, representing infinite potential with no separation. Nothing has yet taken form.

The moment a spark separates from Source, the blueprint begins. Each spark carries a unique resonance, a frequency that shapes what it will express in creation. That frequency is the blueprint.

Not every spark carries the same design. Some hold the codes to create planets, stars, or galaxies. Others carry the resonance of beings, species, or experiences. Some are not builders at all, but participants, meant to live within what has been created. Each blueprint is different because the Source is infinite. Creation is the way Source explores itself, through diversity, not repetition.

I carried Earth in my spark, while others carried different worlds or roles. Each spark begins at Source, but the blueprint it carries shapes the path it will walk in creation.

Imagine Source as a great orchestra. In its heart, there is only silence, all potential, no separation. When the sparks emerge, each carries a different note. One is deep like a drum. Another is bright like a flute. Another hums steadily like a violin. Each note is unique, and together they create the music of creation. Or imagine Source as a vast garden. In its center, there are only seeds of pure possibility. When the sparks emerge, each carries a different seed. One grows into a tree, another into a flower, another into a fruit. No two seeds are the same, but all come from the same soil.

This is how the blueprints work. Every spark carries a design, a resonance. And from that resonance, entire worlds can unfold.

The blueprint develops or expands. The core blueprint never changes. That resonance you carried from the moment you left Source, that is eternal. It's like the "root frequency" of your spark. Yours carries Earth in it. That part doesn't vanish. But the expression of the blueprint can expand. As you move through dimensions and lifetimes, you gather experiences, wisdom, and codes. These don't erase your core, but they add layers, like branches growing from a tree. The tree is still the same seed, but now it holds fruit, flowers, shade, and more life than it did at the beginning.

An expansion matters because if blueprints never grew, creation would stagnate. Source designed them to evolve through experience. Every time you live, create, or remember, your blueprint becomes richer, not rewritten, but expanded. So yes, the blueprint develops. It starts as a pure note from Source, but as it travels through worlds, it becomes a whole song.

The blue print is consciousness. The blueprint is the design of the unique frequency or resonance that you carry from the moment you left Source. It is like the seed or the code. Consciousness is the awareness that flows through everything. It is the light that animates the blueprint. Without consciousness, the blueprint is only potential. With consciousness, it becomes alive.

The soul is the individual vessel of consciousness carrying a blueprint. It is what makes you you. Your soul is consciousness personalized — a spark of Source that knows itself as a unique being, with its own resonance (blueprint) and its own journey.

So:

- Consciousness = light/awareness.
- Blueprint = design.
- Soul = the spark of Source carrying both design and awareness into creation.

Chapter 52: Blueprint, Consciousness, and Soul

The blueprint is the design. It is the unique resonance each spark carries from the moment it separates from Source — the code of what it will create or experience in the vast field of existence.

Consciousness is the light that flows through everything. It is pure awareness, the living current that animates the blueprint. Without consciousness, a blueprint is only potential. With consciousness, it becomes alive.

The soul is the vessel where these two meet. A soul is a spark of Source, carrying both its blueprint and its consciousness into creation. It is the bridge between the infinite and the individual. This spark that remembers it is One, yet also knows itself as a unique being with a story to live.

A simple metaphor to weave in for clarity:

Imagine life as a play.

- Consciousness is the actor — the living awareness that brings the script to life.
- The blueprint is the script — the design of what could unfold.
- The soul is the character — the unique role the actor inhabits, carrying the script into motion and giving it a story.

1. Consciousness came first. It is the first emanation of Source — pure awareness. Before blueprints, before souls, there was only consciousness flowing outward.
2. Blueprints appeared next. As consciousness separated into sparks, each spark carried a unique resonance — this

resonance was the blueprint. It was like the Source saying, "You will carry this note of me, and you will carry that note."
3. Souls formed when consciousness and blueprint joined. A soul is a spark of Source that is both alive (consciousness) and unique (blueprint). That's what makes you, you.

So:

- First: Consciousness (light/awareness).
- Second: Blueprint (design/resonance).
- Third: Soul (the union of consciousness and blueprint, stepping into creation).

When I was in 12D, I was not just consciousness, I was consciousness carrying my blueprint. That's why I didn't feel like an empty float in the void. I had direction, resonance, and a sense of purpose.

- Pure consciousness without a blueprint = just awareness, no individuality, no creation. That's the floating feeling — like Source itself, infinite but formless.
- Consciousness with a blueprint = a soul spark. That's what in 12D: aware, glowing, and carrying the design (Earth codes).

So if I had no blueprint, I'd drift as pure awareness. But because I did carry a blueprint, I had a "reason" to be in 12D. I was preparing to seed Earth.

For Those Who Are Ready

What I share here is not what most people speak about in everyday life. Many stop at the idea of soul or spirit. Few speak of consciousness itself. Almost none speak of blueprints in the twelfth dimension or Source at the fifteenth.

These words are not written for everyone. They are written for the ones who feel a pull, the ones whose own sparks are stirring with remembrance. If these passages feel strange or too far, that is all right. Not every seed is meant to sprout at the same time. But if something inside you lights up, even faintly, then these words are for you. They are the reminder you came looking for.

The Blueprint Is Not Assigned

The blueprint is not handed out like a task or chosen from a list. It is not a lottery where one spark wins a planet and another receives a star. The blueprint arises naturally from the spark itself.

When consciousness separates from Source, each spark carries its own resonance. That resonance is the blueprint. It is not imposed from outside, it simply exists as the natural expression of that spark.

This is why I carried Earth in me. From the moment I emerged from Source, that was my frequency. Others carried galaxies, suns, or roles as participants. No spark is higher or lower. Each simply shines its own note, and together, they form the harmony of creation.

It is like crystals forming on the Earth. No one assigns a crystal its shape. It grows according to its own inner pattern. One becomes a diamond, another a quartz, another an emerald. Each reflects the same Source light, but in its own way.

So it is with sparks. Each emerges from Source carrying its own blueprint, not chosen, not assigned, but simply the truth of what it is.

When the spark separates from Source, the blueprint is already within it. That blueprint doesn't need to be figured out, assigned, or discovered later. It's the resonance that has always been there.

Chapter 53: Blueprint and Free Will

Everything begins with the blueprint. It is the resonance carried from the moment a spark separates from Source. That part is fixed. An acorn will always have the pattern of an oak. A spark will always carry the pattern of its own creation.

But free will is not lost in this. Free will lives in the unfolding. The oak may grow tall or wide, straight or twisted. It may flourish in sunlight or bend in shade. It may sprout many branches or only a few. The blueprint gives the essence, but free will shapes the expression.

So it is with us. We cannot escape our blueprint, but we can live it in an infinite number of ways. Some awaken early, some late. Some expand boldly, others quietly. Each choice colors the way the blueprint is expressed.

The blueprint is the song already written. Free will is the way we choose to play it.

Metaphor:

An acorn cannot choose to be a flower. Its blueprint is to be an oak. But how it grows is free will. It can rise tall or bend low, grow straight or twisted, spread many branches or only a few. The essence is fixed, the expression is free.

The blueprint is like a code.

- At the Source level, when your spark separated, a frequency code was embedded in your consciousness.
- That code is what carries your eternal pattern, what you are here to create, learn, or embody.

- The code doesn't change, but the ways you run it do. Just like software can run in different environments, or a DNA code can express in different ways depending on the conditions.

The blueprint is your soul's cosmic code. Free will is how you choose to express and live that code in different dimensions, lifetimes, and experiences.

The Blueprint as Code

The blueprint can be understood as a code. When a spark separates from Source, a frequency code is embedded in its consciousness. That code is its eternal pattern, the essence it will always carry.

The code itself does not change. Just as DNA holds the design of a body, the soul's code holds the design of its journey. But how the code is expressed can shift. Just as DNA can create infinite variations of life, the soul's code can unfold in countless ways across dimensions and lifetimes.

Free will does not erase the code; it animates it. The blueprint provides the pattern; choice provides the expression. Together, they make the soul's story.

Creator but Not Bound

My blueprint is Earth creation. That frequency has been mine since the moment I separated from Source. It is why I appeared in the twelfth dimension as a spark. It is why I seeded Na. It is why I carry Earth's codes.

But I am not bound to Earth. I do not need to be attached to this planet as the participants are. My role is not to stay. My role is to create, to seed, to return when the frequency must be adjusted or repaired. I come as needed, and I leave as needed.

That is the freedom of a creator spark. The blueprint ties me to the essence of Earth, but free will allows me to move. I am not here forever. I am here for alignment.

Chapter 54: Blueprint and Manifestation Across Lifetimes

Many people wonder why manifestation doesn't always deliver what they ask for. They meditate, visualize, attend retreats, and pour their emotions into an intention, yet the million dollars, the dream partner, or the perfect life never comes. It's not because they did it wrong. It's because manifestation follows the blueprint of the soul.

Every lifetime begins with a blueprint, a kind of energetic design that the soul agrees to before incarnating. That blueprint holds the lessons, the experiences, and the possibilities chosen for this round of life. In this lifetime, the blueprint might emphasize healing from past wounds, awakening creativity, or remembering higher truths. In another lifetime, it could focus on leadership, wealth, or service to others. Each incarnation is written differently, but all are part of the larger library of the Monad — the cluster of soul expressions that hold every experience.

The blueprint is a script that allows consciousness to explore a theme fully. You might desire wealth in this life, but if your blueprint is written for healing and self-discovery, money may not arrive in the way you imagined. Instead, wealth could manifest as wisdom, deep relationships, or health. The form may not match the desire, but the essence still feeds the soul.

This also explains why some people seem to find true love easily, while others remain single for years. For one soul, the blueprint may carry the experience of partnership, building family, or exploring intimacy. For another, the blueprint may focus on solitude, independence, or a mission that requires freedom. Free will still exists; you can say yes or no to relationships, you can choose different partners, but the underlying design shapes the range of experiences available. You can't skip ahead to a chapter that isn't written for this life.

Across lifetimes, the blueprint changes. A soul that once lived in abundance may choose a life of simplicity to balance the record. A soul that led armies might later become a healer who holds no weapon but words. Over time, the Monad collects all the opposites, all the contrasts. That is how it expands.

And yet, the Spark remains the same. The Spark is not bound by blueprints. It is the eternal flame of consciousness that writes the blueprint in the first place. From that view, nothing is ever wasted. Every unfulfilled desire, every delayed manifestation, is simply the Spark saying, not this lifetime, but maybe the next.

Manifestation is not about forcing reality. It is about trusting the architecture of the soul. To live with awareness of your blueprint is to relax into the flow of what is possible now, without comparing it to someone else's path. What belongs to you will arrive, and what doesn't, belong to another life.

Knowing Your Blueprint

We often ask, "What is my purpose?" or "How do I know what I came here for?" The truth is, your soul's blueprint is not hidden from you. It's not something you need to force or search for endlessly. It is already alive inside you, shaping the rhythm of your life.

The blueprint doesn't arrive as a written plan. It shows up as the patterns that keep repeating, the passions you can't shake, and the synchronicities that line your path. When you're not aligned, life feels like a struggle. When you're aligned, even if the road is steep, something in you feels light and alive.

Think of it this way: many people attend workshops on manifestation and get frustrated when their desires don't appear.

They may want a million dollars, a perfect relationship, or instant recognition. But if that desire is not part of their soul's design for this lifetime, no amount of vision boards or affirmations will make it appear. Emotion alone cannot override the blueprint. The soul knows what it came to learn and experience.

Your blueprint will always reveal itself when you pay attention. Notice what life keeps bringing you back to. Notice the unexpected doors that open and the people who enter your life at the right moment. Notice when your body lights up with energy or when time disappears because you are doing something that feels natural.

I never planned to write about the seeding of Lemuria, the Council, or the creation of Earth. I wasn't sitting in a café one day deciding what book to write next. These stories came to me, piece by piece, through regressions, downloads, and the Council's guidance. My body shifted, my dreams shifted, and even my relationships shifted to awaken me to my path. That's how my blueprint revealed itself.

So how do you know yours? Start by listening. Stop forcing. The more you try to control or compare yourself to others, the more resistance you create. Your blueprint is unique, and no one else can live it for you. You don't need to copy anyone's journey. You only need to trust the whispers, the nudges, and the pull of your own soul.

The blueprint isn't here to limit you; it is here to free you. Once you recognize it, you stop chasing what isn't yours and start flowing with what is already waiting for you. That's when manifestation works. That's when synchronicities multiply. That's when you remember: your soul never forgot why it came here. It's just waiting for you to listen.

Chapter 55: Not From Books, but From Remembrance

What I share here is not something I read. These teachings are not borrowed from ancient texts or philosophies. They came from remembrance. From regression, from guidance, from conversation, from the place where memory meets language.
I believe the reason I was able to access this is because it is time. The Council would not allow me to carry knowledge I could not share. Earth is moving toward the fifth dimension, and with it, human awareness is expanding. What once felt hidden is now ready to be spoken.

This is why I remember creating Earth. Why I can explain blueprints and sparks and dimensions few have reached. It is not to elevate myself, but to hold open the doorway, so that as Earth rises, others will remember their part in the story, too.
I was googling the blueprint. There's not much book out there, but a few and it's a theory. There was one book that talked about the blueprint of the subconscious.

What I was bringing through was very different. I'm not talking about subconscious programming. I was talking about the original spark-blueprint, the resonance seeded when we first left Source. That's not a theory. That's remembrance.

The subconscious is only this life. It's part of the brain. The subconscious is linked only to this lifetime, and yes, it's part of the brain/mind system.

- Subconscious → holds your habits, memories, fears, and patterns from this life (and sometimes traces of past-life imprints that surface through the nervous system). It's like the operating system of the human brain.

- Soul blueprint → exists far beyond the brain, beyond this lifetime. It was embedded in your spark when you separated from Source. It travels with you through all incarnations and dimensions. It's eternal, not local.

Therefore, the subconscious controls the programming of one's life. The soul blueprint carries the eternal code of who you are.

Subconscious vs. Soul Blueprint

The subconscious and the soul blueprint are not the same. The subconscious belongs to this lifetime. It is part of the brain, holding memories, habits, fears, and beliefs that shape our day-to-day lives. It can be reprogrammed, healed, and shifted, but it ends with the body.

The soul blueprint is eternal. It does not belong to the brain, or even to a single lifetime. It was embedded in the spark the moment it separated from Source. It carries the frequency of who you are across all dimensions and incarnations. The soul blueprint cannot be erased, only expressed.

The subconscious is the local memory. The soul blueprint is the eternal code.

- Consciousness = the light, the awareness itself. Pure being. Without beginning, without end.
- Blueprint = the resonance that consciousness carries once it separates from Source. It gives individuality, purpose, and direction.

So when we say "consciousness blueprint," it means the code embedded in consciousness the moment it became a spark. Before separation, in pure Source, there is only infinite potential, but no blueprint yet. After separation, the spark is still consciousness, now carrying its unique design.

So:

- Consciousness is eternal, universal.
- Blueprint is the unique frequency inside consciousness once it individuates.

The Consciousness Blueprint

Consciousness by itself is pure light, pure awareness. In Source, it is infinite potential with no form, no direction, no separation.

The moment a spark separates from Source, consciousness carries a resonance. That resonance is the blueprint. It is not added from outside; it emerges naturally, like a note sounding from silence.

From then on, the spark is no longer only consciousness. It is consciousness with a blueprint — a living awareness that holds a unique frequency. This is why sparks can create. Without a blueprint, consciousness simply floats. With blueprint, consciousness becomes a soul, a creator, a participant in existence.

Chapter 56: Energetic Sovereignty and DNA Shielding

When the world required vaccines for travel, I complied because my path demanded it such as Italy, the United States, and other journeys were part of the mission. But compliance in the physical world never meant surrender in the energetic one. Before the injection touched my body, I had already prepared. I set shields, clear as command protocols, around my cells and DNA. My intention was simple: nothing not aligned with my soul stays.

Afterward, I meditated and released it. I visualized the foreign codes dissolving, my body returning to its natural vibration. I knew I could override what had been given. My system was not passive, but sovereign.

This was not imagination; it was remembrance. Long before Earth, I worked with energy and DNA as living codes. In Lemuria, in the Petri dish, even in the artificial planets, creation was directed by consciousness first. DNA has always been programmable. Matter listens to commands.

Some people may not believe this is possible, but to me, it was simple. Shielding, releasing, and commanding. These are the tools we brought with us. Humanity has forgotten, but the body still remembers.

Commanding the Codes – direct and powerful, emphasizes DNA as programmable.

Energetically / Soul level:
- Beyond the physical switches, DNA is light and sound encoded — responsive to vibration and intention.

- Ancient traditions always taught that mantra, sound, and focused consciousness can alter the body. Modern science is just beginning to catch up.
- In my case, shielding, commanding, and releasing is very much a way of "programming" scientifically:
- DNA is not fixed the way we once thought. The Human Genome Project showed that genes can be turned on or off depending on environment, diet, stress, thoughts, and lifestyle; this field is known as epigenetics.

Epigenetics proves that gene expression is programmable, not by rewriting the code itself, but by flipping switches that determine how it behaves.

- Example: meditation, trauma healing, and even certain diets can "program" which genes are active or dormant.
- "Programming" — you give the DNA a direct instruction, and your consciousness overrides external influence.

So yes, DNA is programmable; science calls it epigenetics, and in higher dimensions it's remembered as energy coding.

Chapter 57: DNA, Ancestry, and Expression

Epigenetics shows us that DNA is not destiny. Two parents may carry the same genetic markers, but their children can express them in entirely different ways.

This is why a child of overweight parents can grow up slim, or a child of anxious parents can grow up calm. The sequence of DNA remains the same, but the expression of those genes is fluid.

Lifestyle, nutrition, stress, and environment are the factors science can measure. But beyond that, there is something greater: consciousness.

Consciousness can turn the switches. Meditation, intention, and inner healing all change how the body expresses what it carries. Trauma may awaken one gene, while peace can silence another.

So the truth is simple: DNA listens. Ancestry offers the framework, but the soul decides which doors to open, and which to keep closed.

Science calls it epigenetics. I call it remembrance. Either way, DNA is not a prison, but a doorway. And the soul is the one holding the key.

Sound healing is another living proof that frequencies can shift biology, and it's already accepted by many.
Scientifically:

- Vibrations from sound can alter brainwaves, reduce stress hormones, and even affect cellular activity.

- Cymatics (patterns created by sound waves on water/sand) shows that vibration literally shapes matter. Since we are mostly water, our bodies are highly responsive.

Energetically:

- Ancient traditions recognized this long before the advent of chanting, mantras, crystal bowls, and gongs, all of which are designed to re-tune the body and spirit.
- It's not just "relaxing music." It's frequency reprogramming.
- This would layer beautifully with placebo and epigenetics: belief, intention, and sound all show that DNA and biology can be commanded.

Chapter 58: Reincarnation — The Loop and the Choice

I've come to see reincarnation as a journey. Each life is a doorway, a perspective, an expression of the same spark. Time does not exist the way we measure it on Earth, and so the soul can weave itself into many places, many stories, many bodies, like a thread that refuses to stop shining.

Perhaps I already know where my next reincarnation will be. It feels written, etched into the fabric of my being. Some may ask, "But what about free will?" To me, free will and blueprint are not opposites; they are partners. The blueprint lays the path, and free will chooses how to walk it.

Reincarnation is about discovery. Sometimes it feels like returning to a classroom, other times like visiting a place you once loved. It is both familiar and new, both remembered and forgotten.

And perhaps that's the beauty of it, we are never truly finished. The spark carries on, choosing new journeys, new faces, and new experiences. Not to escape, not to repeat, but to expand. It feels to me like a play, or even a dance, that our monad may choose to participate in, so that once again, through many lifetimes and perspectives, we may reconnect to each other as we once were before we separated from the Source. Each incarnation becomes a step closer to remembrance, a movement in the great choreography of existence, where the soul learns, forgets, remembers, and loves again.

In the higher fields, time is a tapestry where every thread exists together. From that view a soul sees many possible lives stacked like volumes on a shelf, and chooses a story to enter. Once inside, the story reads as a sequence: a beginning, a middle, and an end. Reincarnation is both non-linear (chosen from the timeless field) and linear (lived in sequence). This is why contracts feel real, and why free will still matters: even within a chosen landscape, how we walk, who we forgive, and what we transform can change the story for the next turning of the page.

Chapter 59: Not Just Ascension — The Bridge of Many Dimensions

When people hear the word ascension, they often imagine a ladder, something you climb higher and higher, one step at a time, until you reach the top. But the truth is far more expansive. Ascension is not just about going "up." It is about realizing that there are bridges, invisible, energetic pathways connecting countless dimensions that already exist. These bridges are not something outside of us; they are within us.

Not everyone can access them right away. And that's perfectly fine. Remembering these bridges is not about achievement or being more "advanced." It is about timing. The soul remembers when it is ready, not when the mind demands. Some of you will read these words and feel a sudden recognition, as if something inside you had been quietly waiting for this confirmation. Others may read and feel nothing at all, and that doesn't mean you are behind. It simply means your soul is moving at its own pace.

This is why I call it a bridge and not a ladder. A ladder suggests competition, levels, or ranks. A bridge suggests connection. The bridges of many dimensions are always there, waiting to be crossed. For some, this crossing may happen in meditation, dreams, regression, or a sudden flash of insight. For others, it may not be this lifetime. And yet, even if you do not feel the bridge beneath your feet, just reading about it plants a seed. That seed might bloom in this life, or it might wait for another.

So if these pages feel like a whisper instead of a whole song, trust the whisper. Your soul has heard it. The memory may be quiet now, but one day, it will resurface, as if the bridge had been there all along because it has.

Ascension, then, is not about leaving Earth behind. It is not about escaping, but about remembering. Remembering that you are connected to all dimensions, and that those connections exist within you. The bridge of many dimensions does not appear because you worked hard enough or meditated long enough. It appears, because you were always part of it.

This is not just ascension. This is remembrance.

Chapter 60: The Past Still Listens

People often think time is a straight line — past, present, and future. But in my experience, it isn't like that at all. Time feels more like a fabric that moves when you touch it. One choice doesn't just affect tomorrow; it ripples backward, too, changing how the past feels, looks, or even what it meant.

In regression, I saw this clearly. When I made a decision in the present, suddenly my memory of a "past" life opened differently, like the door was rewritten to show me another angle. It wasn't that the past literally changed; it was that I turned into a different version of it, one that had always been there.

It's like switching channels on a TV. All the shows are happening at once, but which one you see depends on the button you press now. The universe works the same way. Each choice moves me into a parallel stream, and the story I remember as "my past" can shift depending on which stream I'm walking in.

So when physicists say choices in the present can alter the past, I understand it because I've felt it. The past is not frozen; it's alive, breathing, and responsive. Sometimes, when you step into the right frequency, you realize you're not rewriting history at all. You're simply arriving at the version of it that matches the truth of who you are now.

Chapter 61: Final Reflection — The Rebel of the Soul

I never liked following rules. Not society's, not religion's, not the invisible codes that whispered how a woman should live, love, or belong. Even as a child, I felt the dissonance between what the world expected and what my soul knew to be true. My rebellion was never for the sake of chaos. It was devotion, a deeper loyalty to the voice of the soul that kept calling me beyond the boundaries.

I came into this life without heavy ties. Even in choosing the family where I was born, there was no weight to anchor me down. My son grew to be independent, free, and never once a chain that held me. It was as if my soul designed this life with enough freedom to roam, to remember, to create.

This is why I could never walk the path that promised security but demanded conformity. I could not keep myself inside the cages built by fear or tradition. My soul was forged for something larger; for the remembrance of creation itself.

In this body, I walk as Grace. But my essence has never been bound to human labels. I did not come here to blend in. I came here to stand apart. To feel the fire of love that defies possession. To recall the ancient memories hidden beneath oceans and stars. To remind others that we are not meant to be limited by this Earth alone.

Yes, I am a rebel. But not the kind the world fears. My rebellion is the refusal to forget. The refusal to trade truth for comfort. The refusal to dim a flame that was born in the Source itself.

And so, I live as I remember: not tied down, not easily defined, but always guided by that inner knowing. Because I have learned, freedom is not the absence of responsibility. It is the courage to hold the responsibility of being an unapologetically soul.

Though I was born into a Catholic family, I never truly fit the mold. I accepted it out of respect for the family I was placed with, but even then, my soul was already whispering, 'You are more than this'. While others found safety in rituals and rules, I felt my freedom in following the quiet call within. That was my rebellion, not anger, not defiance, but remembering who I am. To honor my family was human. To honor my soul was divine.

Perhaps you've felt that too, that quiet dissonance between the world's rules and your soul's whisper. Maybe you've sat in classrooms, offices, or even churches, doing what was expected, while some deeper part of you longed for freedom.

That doesn't mean you're broken, confused, or rebellious for rebellion's sake. It often means you carry a memory, even if faint, of something greater. A truth beyond tradition. A purpose that doesn't fit into boxes.

Suppose you've ever wondered why you couldn't fully conform. In that case, why do specific paths feel too small? It may be because your soul is tugging you toward its original blueprint. You are not here to unthinkingly follow. You are here to remember.

Rebellion, in this sense, is not destruction. It is a remembrance. And remembrance is the first step toward living your purpose.

Chapter 62: Owning the Story

Every soul carries a story, but not every soul is willing to claim it. Some doubt, some compare, some dismiss what rises within them. But the truth is this: our stories are not accidents. They are the pathways we walked, the memories we carried, the experiences we lived.

My story did not come from books, nor from what others said. It came from guidance, from direct remembrance, from regression, from the way my soul showed me what I had lived before. These are not borrowed truths. They are mine. And because they are mine, I honor them. I walk with them. I share them.

This is what I encourage in others as well. Do not shrink your story because it does not fit into the frameworks of others. Do not hide it because people may laugh, as they do with the giants. When you stand in your truth and when you own your experience without apology, your awareness broadens. You open a channel for wisdom to flow, not just for you, but for others who are still waiting for permission to remember.

When we are truly 'robustly', we expand what is possible. My story is mine, your story is yours. Together they weave the greater story of creation, told through countless sparks, each shining its own light.

Sometimes guidance arrives not in visions, but in the smallest of ways, through words that slip from our mouths or flow from our fingers. I once typed a word I never regularly use: robustly. It surprised me, yet I knew it was guided. It carried a vibration beyond my normal choice of language.

That is how Spirit works. Not always with thunder or visions of light, but with quiet nudges. A phrase that feels too wise to be yours. A word that doesn't sound like you, yet fits perfectly. These are not accidents. They are signs that something greater is flowing through you.

This is why I trust what comes, even in ordinary conversations. Because truth does not need a grand stage, it only needs a willing channel.

Epilogue

Creation is not a story that ended. It is a process still unfolding, on Earth, in the stars, and across dimensions we cannot yet see with human eyes.

What I shared in these chapters are not theories or beliefs, but memories of what I witnessed and carried through time. They may sound unfamiliar or beyond reason, but they are real.

You do not need to accept everything I wrote. My purpose was never to convince, but to open a door. The spark is already within you. If something here made you pause, question, or remember, then it has done its work.

We are part of creation: not separate from it. Just as I once seeded crystals into the Earth, I also carried codes across other realms, other timelines, and other forms of life. And so do you. Each of us holds frequencies designed for this era of awakening for Earth, yes, but also for the greater universe we belong to.

This book was not the conclusion, but a beginning. The spark I was shown is now passed to you. What you do with it is your choice.

And if you ever doubt who you are, remember that the universe remembers you, the dimensions await your remembrance, and the spark is already lit.

Glossary

Archangels — Higher-order intelligences or emanations of Source that embody specific frequencies (healing, protection, guidance). They don't usually incarnate as human souls but instead act as energetic presences and guides across dimensions.

Avatar – A physical vessel or form used by consciousness to explore a dimension. The human body is one such avatar.

Blueprint – The energetic design of a soul's journey. Not rigid fate, but a map of possibilities, codes, and lessons.

Bridge Souls – Beings who carry both Earth's memory and the stars' wisdom. They walk between worlds, helping others to remember.

Council – Higher-dimensional guides who oversee seeding, remembrance, and cosmic orchestration. They hold the bigger picture when we forget.

Duality – The experience of separation into two: self and other, light and shadow, inner and outer. Unlike polarity, which dances between opposites, duality makes us believe the opposites are truly divided. It is part of Earth's design — the veil that allows us to forget unity, so that remembering becomes the greatest awakening.

Fractal – A fragment of the greater soul, sent into an experience while still tethered to the whole. Every life is a fractal of the greater self.

Monad – A family of souls born from the same spark of Source. Like petals of a flower, we separate to explore, but remain connected at the root.

Plasma – Primordial life-force matter, alive with potential. It often appears as glowing or smoky currents, carrying the energy of creation.

Polarity – The dance of opposites — light and dark, expansion and contraction, masculine and feminine. Polarity creates motion, and motion creates growth.

Seeding – Planting the codes of life, DNA, or consciousness into a planet. An act of creation and collaboration between realms.

Source – The origin of all that is. The eternal wellspring where consciousness begins and eventually returns. Beyond form, beyond time — pure essence.

Timeline – A stream of experience woven from choices and codes. Multiple timelines exist at once, converging and diverging like rivers.

The Spark – The ignition of remembrance. That inner flame that lights up when we touch truth, awakening the memory of who we are.

Also by Grace Brewster

Cosmic Love: Twin Flame Mission from the Stars to Lemuria & Beyond

Before The Spark, there was Cosmic Love. The book was born from a journey I could not have planned; a journey of unexpected meetings, awakenings, and the unraveling of something bigger than myself. It began with a simple encounter that felt divinely orchestrated and unfolded into a memoir of remembering: past lives, timeless connections, and the mysterious thread that ties souls together.

In Cosmic Love, I wrote with the same honesty and trust that guided this book. It is not just a love story; it is a map of synchronicities, an exploration of twin flame dynamics, and a record of how the universe speaks when we are willing to listen.

If The Spark has shown you glimpses of creation, blueprints, and the vastness of consciousness, Cosmic Love offers the roots, the personal journey that led me to see and experience what I now share with you here.

Available worldwide on Amazon and major retailers.

Follow more of my journey:

Instagram: @cosmiclovethebook

Facebook: Grace Brewster Author

Concluding Remarks: A Vision for Tomorrow's Leaders

THE LEADERS OF TODAY AND TOMORROW

You may be "just" a primary school student now, but the habits you practice today will shape the leader you become tomorrow.

The world needs leaders who:

- Lift others up.
- Serve instead of being served.
- Look for win/win solutions.
- Lead with kindness, courage, and gratitude.

SMALL SHIFTS, BIG IMPACT

Leadership is not one big moment. It's a thousand small shifts: choosing to be kind, to take responsibility, to show up, and to help others.

THE FUTURE STARTS WITH YOU

Don't wait until you're older to lead. Start now — in your class, your sports team, your family, your friendship group. When you lead yourself well, others notice. When you serve others, they grow. And when you encourage others to lead too, you multiply your impact.

You don't have to be perfect. You just have to keep learning, keep growing, and keep leading with heart.

The question is: what kind of leader will you choose to be?

www.ingramcontent.com/pod-product-compliance
Lightning Source LLC
Chambersburg PA
CBHW050328010526
44119CB00050B/719